AWAKENING
TO THE
Spiritual
Gangsta
WITHIN

AWAKENING TO THE
Spiritual
Gangsta
WITHIN

SHANNON SHIPP

Awakening to the Spiritual Gangsta Within

Copyright © 2023 Shannon Shipp

www.anchoredsoultherapy.com

ISBN 979-8-9895312-3-3

First published in United States of America 2023 by Anchored Soul Therapy

Cover by Shannon Shipp Set by Shannon Shipp

Printed in the United States

Table of Contents

Special Thanks to

YOU

You're amazing. I'm so proud of
you for investing in yourself!
Thank you for trusting me as
your guide while you
Remember Who You Are.

When we allow ourselves to become genuinely **CONNECTED** to who we are, we begin to **REFLECT** on our life, **TRANSFORMING** ourselves, our being, and our life as we **TRANSCEND** for our highest good.

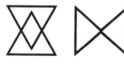

Connect. Reflect. Transform. Transcend.

 # Introduction

Welcome to the closing of 2023, where I find myself living authentically and free from the emotional and subconscious burdens of my past. Today, I proudly embrace my true self and fearlessly share my journey with you. It's essential to understand that I'm not flawless nor a mere victim of circumstances. At various points in my life, I've played the role of both perpetrator and victim. I've made regrettable choices, deceived others, and caused harm. Simultaneously, I've been on the receiving end of betrayal, abuse, manipulation, and unspeakable traumas. I've battled internal struggles like attempted suicide and postpartum depression, all while silently pretending everything was fine.

But amidst the darkness, there arose within me a profound longing for change, a yearning to transform my life for the better. What sets me apart from those still trapped in an unfulfilling existence is my unwavering commitment to personal accountability.

It's worth noting that different perspectives may shape the narrative surrounding my journey. However, I've reached a point where I no longer concern myself with others' perceptions. The stories of my past pale in comparison to the vibrant new chapters I'm crafting for myself. In this fresh life, I've discovered genuine happiness, contentment, and inner peace. Instead of holding onto grudges, anger, or pain, I've chosen to embrace compassion, love, and healthy boundaries.

Let me assure you that sharing my story is not an exercise in blame or a plea for sympathy. Rather, it serves as a glimpse into the transformative power that can arise even from the deepest traumas. It demonstrates that joy can be found in a life once consumed by darkness and despair. My only hope is that those who read these words and yearn for change will find the inspiration and motivation they seek.

Please keep in mind that this book serves as a guide to the tools and strategies that have helped me change my life. During the challenging journey of self-exploration, it is often invaluable to have the support of a professional therapist. The path of shadow work is not easy—it can be dark and frightening at times. Rest assured, I am here to assist anyone in their own shadow work, and you can find my contact information below. Additionally, don't hesitate to reach out to people you trust or seek professional help. Remember, you are not alone, and your well-being matters greatly.

Shannon Shipp
AnchoredSoulTherapy.com
Shannon.AnchoredSoul@gmail.com

Chapter 1
Understanding Change

Why I Wanted Change

Nothing Changes
if Nothing Changes

Before reaching the point I am at today, I was much like the majority of people, simply going through the motions of daily life without experiencing the fulfilling existence I had always yearned for. I immersed myself in work and focused solely on external achievements, mistakenly believing that hard work alone would lead to happiness. I perceived happiness as something external, beyond my grasp. Life seemed to be a continuous cycle of trials and errors, with new challenges always looming. I convinced myself that a miraculous life was not meant for someone like me, constantly comparing myself to others and wondering, "Why not me?"

Have you ever felt that way? Like you were undeserving of living the life you dream of? Like your life was destined to be uninspiring?

It took hitting rock bottom and enduring the darkest days to jolt me awake. Each time I looked in the mirror, I echoed the negative words that others had spoken to me. Love, in its truest form, eluded my comprehension, and the concept of unconditional love remained foreign to me. Something had to change. I confronted my denial and embarked on a journey of self-love. I realized I no longer wanted to be a victim. I craved a life filled with purpose.

In that moment, I began questioning everything, delving deep into the reasons behind my emotions and behaviors. Something had to change if I wanted change. So I began asking myself the hard questions. Why was I allowing the perceptions, judgments, and actions of others to steer me towards darkness and self-loathing? What was the essence of genuine happiness and, most importantly, what was love?

Through consistency and the transformative practices I share in this journal, I brought about profound changes in my life. It became my daily mission to cultivate self-awareness. By being fully present in each moment, I became attuned to my emotions, desires, and thoughts. With each passing day, I gained the power to consciously shape the course of my life. Remarkably, my existence flourished in ways I had never imagined possible, all within a relatively short span of time.

I learned to Unconditionally Love Myself and Others.
I learned my Self Worth and Gained Confidence.
I learned to Self Validate and Healed Codependency.
I learned what Love Meant, Looked, & Felt like to me.

I learned the art of unconditional self-love and extended it to others. I discovered my inherent self-worth and blossomed with newfound confidence. I embraced self-validation and embarked on a journey of healing from codependency. I unraveled the multifaceted meaning, appearance, and sensation of love, as defined by my own unique perspective.

Now, I am living in alignment with the purpose of my soul, immersed in bliss. With this book, my intention is to help you awaken to your own innate joy. This book outlines the most impactful daily practices I embraced to gain these new perspectives and more. These intentional rituals enabled me to unearth the misconceptions I held about myself and my life while dismantling the limiting beliefs that had kept me trapped. These practices guided me toward the love I had always felt was absent within me.

By incorporating this knowledge into your daily routine, you too can experience the profound results on your own

Journey of Rediscovering Your Divine Nature.

THE PAST

Chapter 2
A Trip Down Memory Lane

A Tale of Birth, Resilience, and Triumph.
Childhood Bonds and Struggles
Grooming and Manipulation
Struggling with Relationships and Escaping the Pain
Isolation and Unbearable Secrets
Lessons Beyond the Classroom
Suffering in Silence
Navigating Relationships and Unexpected Realizations
Reckless Choices - The Roaring Twenties
Journey of Healing
In the Depths of Despair
Love and Healing
A Painful Realization
Lessons Learned and Moving Forward
The Meaning Behind Changed Names

A Trip Down Memory Lane

A Tale of Birth, Resilience, and Triumph

The sounds of labor pains and anxious whispers filled the crowded hallway of the hospital, setting the stage for a remarkable tale of courage and unexpected turns. In that chaotic environment, my mother lay on a hospital bed, eagerly awaiting my arrival, while other women in labor shared the same cramped space, each hoping for their miracle.

Despite the slow progression of her labor, my mother remained determined not to succumb to screams. Little did she know that holding back was causing undue stress on both herself and the baby, hindering the natural course of labor. Recognizing the need to intervene, the doctor administered "Twilight sleep" medication. This peculiar drug lulled her into relaxation between contractions, only to awaken her to the piercing pain, leading to momentary unconsciousness.

As her labor continued, my mother faced another unexpected twist. The doctor informed her that she needed her water broken to facilitate progress. To her surprise, the procedure brought an excruciating sensation, leaving her unsure if such pain was expected or not. The doctor then left the room, casually mentioning his return to check on her later.

However, fate had other plans. The moment he stepped away, a nurse's shriek pierced the air, summoning the doctor back in an instant. Panic ensued as they rushed around my mother, urging her not to push while simultaneously attempting to place her on a cart to wheel her into the delivery room. But her body, governed by its primal instincts, defied their pleas, and she gave birth in the hallway, just a few strides away.

Amidst the flurry of activity, my mother drifted in and out of consciousness, oblivious to the commotion around her. Unbeknownst to her, I didn't cry when I entered the world. Instead, medical professionals worked diligently on me, withholding information from my mother.

They whisked me away, urgently attending to a life-threatening situation that had unfolded. The placenta had detached from the wall of the uterus, causing my tiny lungs to fill with blood. Swift action was required as they inserted a tube down my throat to pump out the perilous fluid. The speed at which my delivery occurred proved fortuitous, for had it taken place outside the hospital, survival would have been uncertain.

Regrettably, my mother was denied the joy of holding me and taking me home. Instead, I had to remain in the hospital for a few more days, grappling with the agony of leaving without her baby after enduring the trials of childbirth. The emotional turmoil of that experience was unparalleled.

Yet, amidst this tale of unexpected twists and heart-wrenching separation, there is a glimmer of hope. It is a story of resilience and a baby's miraculous survival against all odds. It is a testament to the strength of the human spirit. Through the darkness and uncertainty, a resilient spirit

My first breath may have been a struggle, but it ignited a flame within me - a flame that would burn brightly, defying the odds and illuminating the path ahead.

This story of my birth serves as a reminder of the fragility of life, the resilience of the human spirit, and the boundless strength that can arise even from the most challenging circumstances.

A Stranger's Intrusion: The Early Years

Most of us don't have any memories from the first three to four years of our lives – in fact, we tend to remember very little of life before the age of 7. And when we do try to think back to our earliest memories, it is often unclear and fragmented. Many believe it's because the hippocampus, considered to be responsible for forming memories, is still developing until at least the age of seven.

However, unlike many others, I possess fragmented memories from the tender age of four. These memories were of my older brother and I at our father's house on the pull-out sofa, watching Paul Bunyan cartoons on Saturday morning. I remember the preschool, The Little Dude Ranch I went to, where I broke my arm trying to go on the horseshoe swings even after being told not to. I also remember being in recess and being made fun of because of my inability to do a split.

Yet, the most haunting memory from age four is the sad scene of my brother and I in our shared room when our mother broke the devastating news of our father's passing. I can still visualize her kneeling, meeting my brother's tear-filled eyes as he struggled to grasp the reality.

Little did I know that this moment would play a pivotal role in my healing journey.

As life settled into a new normal following my father's passing, my mother remarried. This union brought two more siblings into our family. Sundays became a cherished occasion for extended family, cousins, and friends to gather, relax, and enjoy each other's company.

One weekend, during a public event where friends and family mingled, something sinister unfolded. I found myself playing with other children, hopping between the tailgates of two trucks. Suddenly, a stranger approached, seemingly joining in on the fun, but his actions turned disturbing. While helping us jump across, he violated my boundaries, touching my private parts. The discomfort halted my play, and I can only recall fragments of that day.

My next memory is returning home, where my parents invited people for drinks and cards. To my horror, the man from the tailgate arrived, too. My mom put me and my siblings to sleep. I woke up to this stranger in my room at my bed and touching me. Although I only have faint memories of this event, fortunately I do remember, my mother and stepfather caught him in the act and handled the situation..

Childhood Bonds and Struggles

Before my father's passing, my mother and my father's brother began dating. A year or so later, after his passing, they got married, which meant that I continued to be a part of my father's side of the family by spending time with them at family gatherings, which they held every Sunday. My father came from a large family, so the family gathering were filled with laughter and drama. Amidst the chaos, I found myself naturally drawn to my cousin, Catherine, who was close in age to me. We were born exactly three weeks apart, and looking through old photographs, you would see countless pictures of us together. Whether at the beach, at my mom's house, or during holidays, we were inseparable. Catherine was more than just my cousin; she was my best friend.

Yet, I couldn't help but perceive Catherine's life as better than mine, as if she possessed everything I longed for. When I would go over Catherine's house she would always have freinds visit or call and seemed to attract friends who genuinely liked her effortlessly, and I yearned to be more like her. Internally I didnt feel like I measured up. Our bond remained strong, but even within our closeness, specific memories stood out. I recall a sleepover for Catherine's birthday, which coincided with Halloween, so it was a dress up birthday party. At this party I became the target of pranks after falling asleep first. While these incidents hurt my feelings, they were seemingly harmless in the context of childhood antics.

As I entered fifth grade, the onset of puberty brought changes that affected my friendships. Suddenly, my girlfriends displayed both kindness and cruelty. They would be amicable towards me one moment, only to belittle and make derogatory remarks about me in front of boys. I vividly remember walking through the hallways, and with their passing, they would take pincushions and poke them at my breast, stating that they were water balloons and then claiming I stuffed my bra since the balloons didn't pop. While in the bathroom, the girls would gather in the mirror, chanting, "We must, we must, we must increase our bust!" I was puzzled by their actions but desperately wanted to fit in, so I mimicked their arm movements and chants, only to be scolded for doing so.

Throughout my early years, my mother tirelessly worked to improve herself and provide for us. She juggled multiple responsibilities while pursuing her education. At one point she was delivering papers for the local newspaper. I recall one morning I went with her. We got to the job and had to fold and stuff papers in bags, which i thought was so cool seeing how everything worked. Then we went off to deliver the bags of newspapers we loaded into the car. I remember running through the unlit neghborhood yards filled with excitment and being scared at the same time. All it took was one dog bark and I was done for. This would not be the job for me.

Meanwhile, my stepfather, often exhausted from working nights, slept or grappled with anger issues exacerbated by alcohol. The memory of his explosive temper leading to toxic fighting, coupled with frequent relocations, remains etched in my mind. I recall one night when my mom and stepfather's argument escalated so high my stepfather threw a glass ashtray and smashed a lamp. Leading to my mother waking me and my siblings up for a sudden move in the dead of night.

Grooming and Manipulation

On my 10th birthday, my sibling's father helped throw me a birthday party at the park, with most of my aunts, uncles, grandmother, and cousins in attendance. It was a special day, and something unique happened that year. My mother and my sibling's father purchased the same birthday card for me, which was a funny coincidence. I still have those cards saved as a memento.

It was also around that time when my mother introduced us to the man she had been seeing, Iago. Little did we know that he would become a significant presence in our lives for the next eight years.

Iago seemed to bring happiness to my mother's life and treated her with respect, which I hadn't witnessed before. Previously, I had seen my mother cry, struggle, and fight with my sibling's father. So, witnessing her happiness instilled a deep desire to keep her happy. I didn't want to be the reason for her losing it.

Not long after my mother and Iago started living together, my oldest brother, at 11, moved out and went to live with our grandmother. I used to blame him for his departure, feeling yet another sense of abandonment. With my brother gone, I felt a growing responsibility to care for my younger sister and brother. Moreover, seeing my mother go through depression after my brother's departure, I felt an even more vital need to protect and support her. It was during this time Iago began to groom me.

Iago would buy me things, things that I shouldn't have but something that other kids would think was cool. Cigarettes were a big one. Initially, it was just because, but soon enough, stipulations were attached to these gifts. These stipulations emerged after I had already accepted the "gifts."

One day, as I was riding home in Iago's van, he pointed to a bag he had placed in the door. I instinctively grabbed it and thanked him. Little did I know that this simple act would lead to a disturbing conversation.

Iago said, "I'm always doing things for you, so what will you do for me?"
Confused, I replied, "I don't know; what do you mean?"
He continued, "Since I'm giving you these things, you need to do something for me in return."
Perplexed, I asked, "Like what?"
With a dismissive tone, he replied, "Maybe you'll think of something."

Time passed, and eventually, I found myself alone with Iago. He brought up our previous conversation, asking if I had thought about how I would repay him. I admitted that I hadn't.

Without hesitation, he suggested that I let him touch my breast. Shocked and repulsed, I refused. But he quickly threatened to tell my mom that I was smoking, which would make her unhappy and erode her trust in me, just as she had started to feel happier since my brother left.

Feeling trapped and vulnerable, I stood there, contemplating my options. Eventually, I gave in, allowing him to touch me. He dismissed it as if it were no big deal, saying, "See, you made it such a big deal, and it was nothing."

These disturbing interactions continued, but each one was different. Sometimes, there were gifts involved; other times, he would allow me to hang out with friends, and sometimes nothing would happen at all. But there were also moments when he would make demands, leaving me uncertain and on edge. I never knew what to expect from our interactions, as they were unpredictable and varied.

Struggling with Relationships and Escaping the Pain

While the turmoil at home continued, I faced a different kind of struggle at school. Despite having guys express interest in me and wanting to be my boyfriend, I had no desire for a relationship. The thought of being someone's girlfriend meant engaging in boyfriend-and-girlfriend activities, which I did not want. However, succumbing to peer pressure, I would reluctantly accept their offers, only to break up with them shortly after because I had no interest in even holding hands. Unfortunately, after our breakups, these same guys would spread rumors and lies, claiming they had slept with me. Frustrated and hurt, I began outwardly expressing hate towards others and engaging in fights, hoping it would keep people away from me. I spent most of my days in school in ISS,in school suspension, where they issolated you from the other students.

One night, I sat outside on the sidewalk, mesmerized by a dazzling meteor shower. Suddenly, the lights in the house went dark, and it dawned on me that my mom had forgotten I was still outside. Initially, worry washed over me as I wondered how I would get back inside. However, a realization struck me - the slider on the porch offered an easy way in. Instead of heading indoors, I boldly embraced the newfound freedom and explored the quiet and peaceful neighborhood. The cool air welcomed me, and the silence enveloped my senses. It was a liberating experience.

As I strolled around, a glimmer of hope flickered within me, yearning for a chance encounter with someone. Unfortunately, my hopes were dashed, and I soon found myself back at home. Despite this, a sense of relaxation and exhilaration coursed through me. It was a brand new escape I had discovered. I cherished my freedom.

From that night onward, I couldn't resist the allure of sneaking out. Initially, it felt like escaping the chaos that consumed my mind. However, as time passed, my adventures in sneaking out led me to seek even more thrilling forms of escape. It was during these escapades that I found myself in the homes of older individuals, men in their twenties. Remarkably, I was only twelve or thirteen years old, and these men still found it acceptable to offer me drinks. It was during this time that I first ventured into the world of drinking.

Sneaking out became a regular occurrence until one fateful night when I returned home to find my mom's bedroom light turned on. Panic surged through me, and I immediately knew I had been caught. Ignoring the fact that my bedroom light was off and no other lights were illuminated besides my mother's light, I made the ill-advised decision to peer into my mom's window. In an instant, her piercing scream shattered the night. She had spotted me watching through the window. Initially, she didn't recognize me, but soon realized it was her child. Hastily, she rushed to the back door, calling out for me. I had been found out.

Now I was on lockdown. Dealing with the drama at school and the ongoing abuse at home left me constantly on edge. I despised my life, and the weight of it all became too much to bear. Multiple times, I contemplated ending my own life. One particular instance occurred during my 7th or 8th-grade year when my mom and Lago were not home. In a moment of despair, I entered my mom's room and grabbed her gun. Standing there, staring at my reflection in the mirror, I was ready to leave this world. The gun was pressed against my head when suddenly, one of my siblings pushed open the door, causing me to discard the weapon hastily. I stopped because I thought about the potential consequences for my sister and younger brother if I were no longer around.

Realizing that I couldn't go through with ending my life, knowing I couldn't abandon my siblings, I turned to self-harm as a means of escaping the emotional pain I was enduring. I would take razor blades and cut the insides of my ankles, using lighters to burn my hands, knuckles, and ankles. Even today, I bear a scar on my knuckle from one of those lighter burns. Anything to distract my mind from the overwhelming emotions I felt within.

Isolation and Unbearable Secrets

Shortly after, we moved to the country side of town without neighbors near by, stopping my sneaking-out adventures. My brother is still gone, and I can no longer join my siblings on weekend visits, leaving me alone with my mother and Iago. My mother and Iago embarked on building a livestock farm, and amidst the hard work, I found solace in the presence of the animals. It became an escape for me, a way to avoid being trapped inside.

In the vast expanse of the land we lived on, Iago would invite me to go hunting with him, praising my keen eye and ability to spot things he couldn't. Initially, these outings seemed innocent, devoid of any inappropriate encounters. He made me believe that I was safe. However, over time, these trips turned into dreaded experiences filled with unwelcome touches and coerced actions. Sexual encounters tainted every interaction I had with him, as I realized that it was all a manipulative game.

As the gifts from Iago diminished, his psychological manipulation grew more sinister. He would degrade me, labeling me as disgusting and a whore, incessantly questioning me about my interactions with boys from school. Eventually, he began encouraging me to flirt and attempt to engage in sexual acts with one of his adult male friends.

"Go flirt with him and tell him you want to sleep with him."
I would do so and tell Iago the man didn't respond or wasn't interested. Iago reassured me it was him playing hard to get and told me to keep doing it. Telling me to force myself onto him and promising to leave me alone that day if I did as he said, but it was always a lie. There was always some condition attached, and he would ultimately go back on his word.

Thankfully, his friend ignored my attempts and never responded. However, one day, my mom discovered my diary entries about my crush on this male friend and confronted me, hurling insults and confirming everything Iago had said would happen.

Life felt unbearable and unjust. Why did my faather have to die and be replaced with Iago? The lack of safety that gripped me was so intense that I became terrified to sleep or even move around my own home.

Some may question why I didn't speak up. I often berate myself for this, but I must remember that I was only ten when it all began. I had already experienced sexual assault and witnessed other unhealthy adult interactions. What was normal anymore?

I went from witnessing my mom endure physically and emotionally abusive relationships and financial struggles to seeing her happy and free from financial stress. I couldn't be the one to shatter her happiness. Moreover, with my older brother gone, I had taken on the mental role of protecting my siblings. I couldn't risk leaving the house and leaving my sister vulnerable. I genuinely believed I was protecting everyone.

Lessons Beyond the Classroom

Amidst the turmoil at home, I sought solace within the walls of my school. However, my school life was just as tumultuous as I yearned to escape its unique challenges.

The drama in school followed me into high school, and I became known for my sharp tongue and readiness to fight at a moment's notice. In my locker, I kept steel-toe boots and brass knuckles, symbols of my defiance. To mentally escape, I even stashed vodka, my liquid refuge. I projected an aura of indifference as if I didn't care about anyone or anything - and on the surface, I honestly didn't. I formed a close bond with a girl who saw my anger as her bodyguard. I defended her relentlessly, starting fights with people I didn't know because she claimed they had wronged her. We shared classes and rode the bus together. However, halfway through the year, her cousin moved to town and joined our school. Suddenly, my friend distanced herself from me, and together, they concocted rumors about me. They would get caught smoking in the bathrooms and falsely implicate me to the administrators. They even defaced the bus loop with graffiti that read, "Shannon Shipp is a whore." I couldn't comprehend why they turned on me, but in hindsight, I realized that my "friend" and I had engaged in similar behavior with other girls, so it felt like a twisted normalcy.

Throughout those years, I felt neither safe nor wanted in any aspect of my life. Trust was a foreign concept, and a deep loneliness consumed me. Yet, I wasn't fully aware of this; I masked everything so much that I even had myself convinced everything was normal. I took on the role of the bitch and the girl with an attitude because that where I seemed to fit.

The abuse from Iago persisted. There was always something, a constant torment, that made me yearn for a loving and protective father figure. Secretly, I embarked on a quest to uncover the truth about my natural father and the circumstances surrounding his death. The newspaper clippings painted a picture of a remarkable man - a devoted father of two, a successful tow truck business owner, and a beloved community member who suddenly had everything stolen from him at the younger age of 25. Why would someone commit such a senseless act and take him away from me?

After searching for answers about my father, I became interested in esoteric, spirituality, and witchcraft. I studied and began practicing psychic abilities in my early teens from the books my mother owned. As I struggled to make sense of the pain and emptiness that consumed me, I embarked on a personal journey through the exploration of spirituality.

In the darkest moments of my life, I yearned for something greater than myself, something that could bring solace and meaning to my shattered existence. It was during this period of immense vulnerability that I began questioning the nature of life, the universe, and my place within it. I sought refuge in books, delving into various spiritual philosophies and practices, eager to find a glimmer of hope and understanding.

In my junior year, a new school was opening and I was allowed to transfer to a new high school. Hope surged within me as I anticipated leaving behind the drama that had plagued my previous school. For the most part, I did find respite. However, the same group of girls from the prior school, seemingly bored and lacking purpose, decided to target me. They went out of their way to cause chaos in my life. They vandalized my car on school grounds and even ambushed me while I was walking into work.

To make matters worse, my current group of friends turned against me. One of my long-time friends spread rumors that I was trying to sleep with her boyfriend and attempted to confront me within the school walls. I had no romantic interest in her boyfriend, and I had rejected his advances even before they started dating.

Suffering in Silence

At the tender age of 16, drinking and smoking became my everyday escape from the pain and chaos that surrounded me. Despite my rebellious behavior, I managed to maintain good grades, but my attitude and reliance on alcohol persisted. Fortunately, having my car and a job allowed me to spend less time at home, providing a much-needed respite from the turmoil.

During this time, I found myself becoming pregnant by the guy I had the biggest crush on, a result of a drunken night that I barely remember. Fearful of the repercussions from my mother, who had already labeled me a whore, and Iago's threats of abandonment and homelessness if I became pregnant, I chose to keep the news to myself.

When I finally mustered the courage to confide in my two best friends, they dismissed my disclosure, refusing to believe me. However, one of my friends, Red, offered her support and stood by my decision to get an abortion.

With a doctor's appointment scheduled for the next day, I was working at the customer service desk in Winn Dixie when I suddenly felt something was wrong. Cramps and a familiar sensation signaled the impending start of my period. Our uniforms at Winn Dixie were pristine white, and I knew I couldn't wait out these cramps. In a panic, I asked Red, preparing to end her shift, to cover for me so I could rush to the bathroom. However, she refused, yelling about her impatient grandmother waiting and her delay. Finally, someone agreed to cover for me, and I rushed to the bathroom.

Inside the bathroom stall, I quickly undressed and sat down, only to witness a large lump emerge from my body. Confusion and fear engulfed me as I stared at the bloody mass in the toilet. Without thinking, I flushed it away, overcome by panic and uncertainty. What had I just done? Why did I do that? What do I do now? I had no one to turn to, no one to share my pain with.

After my shift, I went to Red's house, where I was staying overnight in preparation for the abortion appointment the following day. Still unaware of what had transpired at work, I told Red about the incident. She was at a loss for words but assured me everything would be fine after the doctor's visit. The following morning, Red and our other friend, Anne, accompanied me to the clinic. They offered to drive me home after the appointment, dropping me off and instructing me to call them when I was ready to be picked up.

Inside the clinic, I filled out the necessary paperwork and waited to be called back. The nurse eventually led me to a room, instructing me to undress and put on a gown before lying on the table to await the doctor's arrival. As the doctor examined me, she remarked, "You're bleeding." I explained what had happened, prompting her to bring over the ultrasound machine. The ultrasound revealed nothing, leading the doctor to conclude, "Well, you're not pregnant now, so I can't help you." I still had to pay for the appointment, adding insult to injury. I left the clinic and called my friends to pick me up, informing them that the procedure hadn't been performed because I was no longer pregnant. Throughout the car ride home, the girls treated me as though I had fabricated the entire pregnancy, accusing me of lying.

In the weeks that followed, my body poured out blood, accompanied by chunks of tissue. I was forced to sleep sitting up in my bedroom chair, with pads and towels underneath me, as the horrifying experience unfolded. I had no answers, no explanations for what had happened. All I could surmise was that I had miscarried while at work, and in my panic, I had flushed the fetus down the toilet.

Navigating Relationships and Unexpected Realizations

The year I turned 18 was a whirlwind of events, making it challenging to piece together the exact chronological order of these transformative experiences. However, amidst the haze of memories, certain moments stand out vividly.

On my 18th birthday, I was granted permission to have a party at my family's farm. Rather than hosting it indoors, we decided to utilize the barn, which featured a stage, a bar, and an entertainment area. This was a familiar setting for my parents' gatherings. I invited my friends, who, in turn, brought along their siblings and friends. The party was a relaxed affair, filled with laughter, drinks, and good company. At one point, I went to the house to use the bathroom. Little did I know that this detour would change my life.

As I exited the house, I unexpectedly bumped into Yunho, a slightly older guy who had been invited by one of my friend's brothers. Although we had crossed paths before, we had never engaged in much conversation due to his reserved nature. However, at that moment, he opened up to me, expressing his fondness for me and wishing me a happy birthday. To my surprise, he leaned in and kissed me, igniting a spark that would lead to a relationship.

Yunho was a sweet and funny person, albeit passive. Being a few years older than me, he treated me with kindness and respect, and we embarked on a relationship that lasted approximately two years. We shared many memorable moments and built a strong bond.

However, one night, a conversation between Yunho and me took an unexpected turn. He mentioned an ex-girlfriend who had confided in him about being sexually abused by someone close to her. Shockingly, he revealed that he had broken up with her because he couldn't handle the situation, using the term "grossed out" to describe his feelings. At that moment, a profound realization hit me. The person I was in a relationship with felt repulsed by someone else's trauma, and it became clear that our relationship had reached its end. Yet I was not ready to admit my situation or face rejection, so I stayed quiet.

Instead of acknowledging that our relationship was over and realizing that I deserved someone who would stand by me, support me, and empathize with the hardships I had endured, I found myself internalizing even more hurt and rejection.

This realization hit me like a wave, crashing against the fragile walls I had built around my heart. Instead of using it as an opportunity for growth and self-reflection, I allowed the pain to seep deeper into my being. I questioned my worth, wondering why I wasn't enough to inspire compassion and understanding in someone I had cared for deeply.

The rejection I felt from Yunho's response to his ex-girlfriend's trauma echoed within me, amplifying the insecurities and doubts that had already plagued my thoughts. I began to believe that perhaps I was unworthy of love and support, that my own experiences of pain and suffering were too burdensome for someone to bear.

This internalization of hurt and rejection clouded my judgment and self-perception, leading me down a path of self-doubt and emotional turmoil. I failed to recognize that the shortcomings of others did not define my worth or determine my capacity for love and happiness.

The situation with Iago continued until I graduated from high school. One day, while I was out with my boyfriend, my mother called me. She requested that I pick up my sister and brother and take them somewhere but not return home until she gave me the go-ahead. She had discovered some unsettling news about Iago.

As I hung up the phone, a whirlwind of emotions flooded over me—happiness, fear, relief, and anxiety. All those years of staying silent, afraid my mom would be angry with me, were proven wrong. Instead, she stood up for us and did everything in her power to remove Lago from our lives, prioritizing the safety of her children. I realized that I had been foolish for keeping everything to myself. It was time to take action and protect my siblings.

I wish I could say that after that phone call, I never saw Iago again, but unfortunately, that wasn't the truth. My mother immediately kicked him out of the house, ensuring he never returned. However, his actions didn't stop there. He began showing up at my workplace, waiting for me in the parking lot after my shift. He attempted to manipulate me with more lies. Fortunately, I didnt fall for his tactics and immediately informed my mother.

Meanwhile, my relationship with Yunho became increasingly strained as I sought an escape. Being older, I believed he could provide me the relief I sought. I envisioned us moving in together and starting a new life. At the time, he lacked any goals or dreams and seemed content in his early twenties, living with his parents, hanging out with friends, and indulging in drinking and smoking. Due to the abuse I had endured at home, I craved an escape. I would drink excessively until I blacked out or passed out, using intimacy with my boyfriend as a way to numb the pain. I was desperately searching for a way out.

After Iago was exposed and out of the house, I confided in my boyfriend about my situation. His response was lackluster, and our already rocky relationship became even more strained. His parents disapproved of me, and my revelation was the final straw. He ended our relationship. Although I knew we wanted different things in life, his rejection felt like abandonment, and I begged him to reconsider. I oscillated between pleading with him and resorting to extreme measures, such as showing up unannounced at his house and knocking on his windows at night, desperate for his attention.

When Yunho and I were "working things out," I attended a party with some new friends I had recently met, along with my friend Anne. As expected, there was drinking involved. At some point during the night, I was playfully pushed into the pool, fully clothed, and had to change into dry clothes. While I was changing, the party's host entered the room, as I stood there in my underwear and we begun kissing until Anne unexpectedly barged in. Instead of being a supportive friend and getting me out of the room with that guy, she claimed she had called her boyfriend and was leaving. She turned her back and left.

By the time I retrieved my wet clothes from the dryer and managed to dress myself, Anne was long gone. I attempted to call her during my drive home, but her boyfriend answered the calls and argued with me. The worst part came the following day when Anne and her boyfriend contacted all our friends, as well as Yunho, to inform them that I had slept with the guy at the party. This marked the definitive end of my relationship with Yunho and severed all the "friendships" I had within that group. I was utterly cast out and isolated.

Back at home, my mother eventually confronted me about the issues with Iago, which made both of us uncomfortable. Whenever she broached the subject or asked questions, I felt she was interrogating me and doubting my words. I didn't feel trusted or believed. In hindsight, I understand it was incredibly difficult for her as a mother to learn about these things. The confrontation strained our relationship even further, and I found myself turning to drinking as a coping mechanism more and more.

Reckless Choices: The Roaring Twenties

While I was in high school and working at Winn Dixie, a supervisor, Caligula, constantly flirted with me. When I turned 20, I ran into Caligula after the difficult situation with my stepfather ended and the end of my friendship situation. At that time, I was subconsciously seeking an escape from everything and Caligula was my opportunity. He asked me to meet him at some clubs, and this soon became a frequent occurrence, eventually leading to our dating.

With tensions rising at home, I decided to leave with nothing but an overnight bag and started staying with Caligula. Although I didn't technically move in, I spent every night there. This decision led me into a life of drugs and more trauma than I was prepared for.

Being 13 years my senior, Caligula may not have had money, but he was smooth with his words and always found ways to get special treatment. Caligula introduced me to a world of luxury, including limousine rides to mansion house parties, private exclusive nightclubs, and backstage experiences. However, these glamorous experiences were often centered around sex and swingers. Despite this, Caligula always respected my wishes and never forced me to do anything I didn't want to do. My trust in him grew, and as a couple, we would meet people at clubs and parties, with Caligula teaching me how to attract and engage with women and men alike. It became a game and competition for him. Gradually, he convinced me to experiment with ecstasy and Xanax, which wasn't difficult considering my desire for escapism. Eventually, we started hosting parties with strippers and random people from the club. Caligula had a voyeuristic nature and enjoyed watching others.

As time went on, the drugs escalated from lighter substances to harder ones, with Caligula using cocaine. He desired more experiences, even if I wasn't willing to participate, asserting that I hindered his enjoyment of such events. Eventually, he began bringing women home while I was present, entertaining them while I pretended to be asleep. Within a few months, I found myself descending into a dark path, battling depression, struggling to eat, and relying solely on drugs.

One night, as we got ready to attend an after-party after being out all night, I reached a breaking point in our relationship. I expressed my unwillingness to go, but my refusal was not acceptable. Seeking a moment to collect myself, I went into the bathroom; however, instead of freshening up, I made a desperate attempt to end my life by ingesting a large quantity of pills and attempting to harm myself with a kitchen knife. The combination of medications and alcohol left me in a state of confusion. Fortunately, I only inflicted superficial wounds, so the situation wasn't life-threatening.

In my semi-conscious state, I grappled with Caligula because, while I wanted to die, he insisted on going out. He wanted me to accompany him to the party, as he wouldn't be allowed in otherwise. In a twisted attempt to "make me happy," he resorted to raping me, justifying it as something I supposedly needed to feel better. Later, he argued that it couldn't be considered rape since we were in a relationship.

After that incident, I moved back home while still seeking ways to escape. There were many nights I was drinking, influencing my underaged siblings to join me, starting fights with my older brother, and breaking my mother's furniture. I was an absolute mess from not facing the painful emotions that boiled below the surface and showed up as anger.

On one occasion, I attended a party at my cousin Catherine's house with my older brother. By this point, I was no stranger to drinking, and it often made me aggressive. Although I don't remember what I did to upset someone at the party, suddenly, one of my cousin's friends confronted me, accusing me of talking behind her back. I never backed down from a fight, and before I knew it, I was hit and fell to the ground. I quickly got back up and continued fighting until my older brother intervened, pulling me into the car to go home. Reflecting on that memory, I recall Catherine standing in the doorway, watching the fight unfold. After that incident, I didn't spend much time with Catherine or talk to her.

Journey of Healing

Throughout my life, I found solace in the world of art, and in my late teens to early 20s, it was mainly through photography. This passion inspired by my mother's deep affection for capturing moments with her camera. I fondly recall the times I joined her on drives through the picturesque landscapes of Palm Beach, watching her skillfully frame and capture scenes. Waiting for those to develop was like reliving cherished memories.

My enthusiasm for photography only grew during my high school years when I took photography classes. This passion led me to a job at Winn-Dixie, where I began as a cashier but soon transitioned to the photography department. This early experience laid the foundation for my future. I eventually worked in local photography stores, where I honed my skills. It wasn't long before I ventured into my photography business.

I started by building my portfolio, specializing in prom photos and portraits. The confidence I gained allowed me to secure a managerial role at a photography store in the mall, all before the age of 21.

After ending things with Caligula, I met someone new named Huck. Despite crossing paths at a strip club, I wasn't working there; I frequented the place and knew many staff. It served as a spot where I could unwind with a drink, even though I was underage. Huck and I quickly developed a strong bond. He was around my age and embarking on another year of college, and we shared many common interests. A few months into dating, Caligula still bothered me, attempting to return to my good graces.

One night, Huck and I went out with a group of his friends to the strip club where we initially met, and coincidentally, we ran into Caligula. Initially, I planned to leave, but Huck convinced me to stay, assuring me there wouldn't be any issues because we had a large party and people wouldn't let Caligula bother me. Despite my hesitation, I reluctantly went back inside. As it turned out, Caligula left after we returned inside, and we could enjoy the rest of the night. However, when it was time to go, I found my car with the back window busted out and all of my photography equipment and purse stolen. I knew it had been Caligula.

Unfortunately, Caligula eventually found out where I worked and began causing scenes when he entered the store looking for me. I had to involve the police and get a trespassing order against him to make him leave me alone. Around that time, Huck was settling into another year of college in Orlando, and I saw it as my chance to escape the situation. I decided to move in with him, and we settled into his off-campus housing, living with his roommates.

Through my connection with Huck, I started rediscovering myself and healing from the traumas I endured with Caligula. Initially, our relationship was around going out, escaping reality, as we would smoke and drink at home while playing dominos, but the use of ecstasy soon came to an end as he introduced me to the world of plant medicine. On a few occasions you could find Huck and I rummaging through cowfields harvessting mother natures medicine. While we would use this for our own pleasure and escape, at the time, I wasnt aware of how I was mentally being healed through this medicine.

Huck was interested in esoterics and encouraged me to tap into my gifts. The more I explored this realm, the more strange occurrences would happen. One instance that stood out was when Huck came home from classes and found me typing uncontrollably at the computer desk. I was unresponsive until Huck managed to get me to snap out of it, but I couldn't recall what I was doing. Another time, I woke up to find myself choking Huck in his sleep. It was after that incident that I decided I no longer wanted to engage with the spiritual realm. Eventually, we shifted our focus towards exploring plant medicines, such as mushrooms. My family adored Huck, and we maintained a healthy relationship, but deep-seated insecurities about my appearance and his feelings for me lingered.

Around our second year together, we moved to a private home. In due course, we became engaged, even though I was uncertain about marriage and my future. My childhood trauma made it difficult for me to envision starting a family. Nevertheless, I accepted the engagement. When pressured to set a wedding date, I suggested a six-year timeline, as I felt there was no rush. At 21 years old, I was still searching for my life's purpose. However, this didn't meet Huck's expectations, and our relationship grew tumultuous.

Then came my birthday, a day that shattered me. As I sat down at the computer, I discovered an open email from Huck to a woman he worked with, discussing the enjoyable time they had recently spent together. My world crumbled around me as I realized he had cheated on me. The pain was overwhelming, and although I struggled to forgive him, the rage persisted whenever I saw him. We were unable to mend the broken trust, leading us to separate. We attempted to remain friends for a while, but eventually, that, too, ended.

Escaping the Cycle: My Journey From Abuse to Empowerment

I spent some time alone, going out on dates but not meeting anyone interested. At one point, I did consider rekindling things with Huck since we were still friends, but he turned me down, and that was the last time I allowed him to make a fool of me. I thought the next person who came into my life would be different, right? I had experienced a good relationship with a man who loved and treated me well. However, deep insecurities and lacking trust in others and myself persisted. I was determined to find a good relationship.

Then came Ernest. He lived in the same apartment complex as me, and we met in the parking lot one day as I was returning from work. In the beginning, Ernest did and said all the right things. Our relationship was quick and became a roller coaster ride. I remember he lost the lease on his apartment and ended up staying with me for a bit, but I eventually moved to a different apartment without him while we still dated. Ernest had a drinking problem and would often mix alcohol with smoking, which led to verbal and physical abuse towards me.

Whenever we would hang out or he stayed with me, everything seemed great, and we would have fun. But suddenly, things would take a turn. I recall one day when we went fishing, one of his favorite activities. We spent most of the day fishing and drinking, but then I received a call from my cousin, Catherine, inviting us to a party that night. Catherine lived about 2 1/2 hours away, and considering the late hour and our alcohol consumption, I didn't think it was wise to make the trip. However, Ernest took it as if I was embarrassed about him and didn't want him to meet my family. An argument ensued, and I expressed my desire to go home. As it was getting dark, we started packing up. The drive home was tense, with Ernest continuing to drink, smoke, and yell. He became increasingly aggressive, hitting me and banging my head against the car window.

Feeling trapped and desperate, I couldn't bear it any longer. I opened the car door and threw myself out, scrambling to find somewhere to hide in the bushes. From my hiding spot, I watched Ernest park the car and search for me. He came close but didn't find me. Eventually, he grew tired and started walking back to the car. Thinking he was gone, I cautiously emerged from the bushes, intending to walk home. However, out of nowhere, his car reappeared, and he began chasing me. He parked and got out to chase me on foot. I tried to evade him, but he caught up and began hitting me, attempting to drag me back to the car. I slipped and fell into a ditch. Eventually, he left in the car again, and I remained in the gutter, battered and exhausted.

Sometime later, he returned and tried to drag me back into the car. I fought back as much as possible, but he got me inside. Exhausted and defeated, I gave in and stayed in the car. When he got into his side of the car, he slammed my head against the window, knocking me out.

The next thing I remember is waking up in the parking lot to him knocking on the window, asking if I was going to get out of the car and come up to the house. I was confused about what was happening but obliged. While I was unconscious in the car, he had already been in my home, cooked a meal for himself, showered, and was watching TV. All of this while I was sitting in the car, knocked out from him, banging my head against the window.

I don't recall exactly when, but I remember the police visiting at some point. The police had been called by a passing car that witnessed him hitting and shoving me into the car. The person followed us, observed his actions, and reported it to the police. Finally, I could file a police report against him, which was a first because, in previous instances, the police would try to press charges against me instead of him. He would lie to the police, claiming that I was belligerent, hitting myself, or being irrational. Unfortunately, nothing was done since I didn't have any visible marks.

Shortly after that incident, another violent episode occurred. This time, he punched me right in the face, giving me a black eye. I tried to conceal it with makeup when I went to work, but a friend noticed and accompanied me to the police station to file a report.

Thanks to her support, I finally obtained a restraining order against him. I was also enrolled in domestic violence classes, which surprisingly taught me a lot and helped with my self-esteem. It made me realize that what I had been experiencing was not normal.

At this point in my life I was attending school and attempting to find myself. I had no idea what I wanted to do with my life. In order to feel like I was doing something with my life, I was taking some classes in college hoping that would help me figure it out. I continued to attract people who had problems similar to or worse than mine, and each experience seemed to be worse than the one before. I met someone with whom I had constant fights, and he cheated on me regularly. During that time, I was attending school for Graphic Design, but he wanted me to accompany him to a college orientation. Out of support, I went with him, and that's when I discovered Massage Therapy. I had never heard of it before, but I was captivated and decided to drop out of Graphic Design school to pursue Massage Therapy. From that point on, I never looked back.

During this time, I was still silently exploring spirituality and learning more, but my confidence lacked in trusting my intuition. My intuition was quick and fleeting, and I could never back it up with concrete evidence, so the people around me, especially my partners, dismissed me and told me things like, "You're crazy." "You're making things up." So, I kept much of my intuition to myself and, most importantly, didn't trust it.

As our second anniversary approached, we had moved into a new house, but I was struggling to catch up financially after the moving expenses. Given the tight money situation, I didn't think it was logical to go on the planned trip. However, he went anyway, and that's when our relationship ended. I mean, who goes on an anniversary trip without their partner?

When he went on that trip, he left our roommate and me to fend for ourselves, and honestly, it all landed on me. Eventually, the roommate and I were in a relationship, but, looking back, I'm not sure if I would consider it a proper relationship due to his battle with drugs. He spent a lot of time struggling with his demons, and I found myself sacrificing a lot and being alone frequently due to him either being in rehab or jail. At one point, my cousin Catherine graciously took us in as I was trying to stay financially afloat while supporting both him and myself. I am incredibly grateful for her help during that time. It was only a few months before I moved out.

At one point, I was separated from him due to his incarceration, and I resided with my mom. This gave me the opportunity to embark on a journey of self-discovery. It was during this period that I stumbled upon something that compelled me to embrace new experiences and start saying "yes." Until then, I had spent my entire life conforming to the desires of others, losing sight of my own identity. I felt uncertain about who I indeed was and what I genuinely enjoyed. The opportunity to say "yes" felt like a breath of fresh air, liberating me from my self-imposed limitations.

Throughout this personal quest, my mother accompanied me to numerous workshops. One of these workshops, held at a local spiritual store, stands out in my memory. We gathered in a yoga studio, arranged in a half circle around the facilitator. It was there that I was introduced to a book that profoundly impacted me: "The Little Soul and the Sun." This book sheds light on pre-choosing our life experiences before coming to Earth. Even the most challenging situations are purposefully chosen by us. Leaving that workshop, I carried a new perspective that allowed me to change how I viewed the world around me.

Turning the Corner:
Premonitions and Transformation

To escape my previous relationship, I accepted a job with a former employer who generously loaned me money to retrieve my car from repossession and start fresh in a new place. I worked tirelessly, selling stripper clothing, to repay my debts. Eventually, I managed to secure a cute and cozy apartment for myself.

Shortly after settling into my new place, I dreamed of a man holding two baby boys. When I woke up, I felt that this man was someone who would come into my life as my future husband, keeping our unborn children. It was surprising because I wasn't interested in having kids then. A month later, I began talking to someone from an online dating app called OkCupid. I should note that online dating was starting and nothing like today.

After several months of online conversations, I agreed to meet him for lunch. When we met, I was shocked because he was the man I had dreamt about. He approached me wearing a beanie cap, with a light complexion and a handsome face, and he could hold an engaging conversation. He greeted me, introducing himself to Pepe. He had recently moved from Puerto Rico, and his noticeable accent was the icing on the cake for me. I was captivated by Pepe's presence.

When we met, I had already graduated from massage school and was working a job while running my own side business. I was privately exploring spirituality. One of our first dates was going to a psychic, which was a unique experience for me. Through that psychic, I met influential mentors as they worked at her shop. Pepe encouraged me to delve deeper into my spirituality.

When Pepe and I first met, I was still drinking, and I was amazed that I had made it to my 30th birthday, considering the circumstances I had been through. To celebrate, I went on a cruise with my mother and younger siblings. Although there was a lot of fun, I acknowledge that my drinking sometimes caused me to behave poorly. Soon after that experience and during my relationship with Pepe, I realized I needed to quit drinking. I wanted to have better experiences and relationships, and Pepe pointed out that my drinking behavior was out of control. So, I decided to quit drinking.

A Rollercoaster of Revelations: Making Life-Altering Decisions

At the beginning of our relationship, I was deeply immersed in exploring my spirituality. During this time, I stumbled upon a Reiki class and felt a strong pull to attend. Excited by this newfound interest, I invited my mom, who shared a similar passion for spirituality, and Pepe to join me in this experience. Together, we embarked on a journey to deepen our understanding of energy healing and I hoped it was a way for Pepe and I to deepen our bond.

Although we had some great moments, Pepe was emotionally inconsistent, fully present when we were together but distant when we weren't. Ignoring the red flags, I was determined to prove my premonition right. During a visit to my sister, who had just had her third son, I yearned for a baby, possibly due to my adorable nephew reaching my thirties.

In my premonition, I envisioned the conventional path to happiness: a husband and children. I disregarded the red flags because I believed that love was difficult and men were prone to cheating. By October 2012, our relationship became a rollercoaster of breaking up and getting back together. Iparticipated in a breast cancer 5K with my co-workers, including a pregnant colleague. Strangely, I found myself needing to use the bathroom every time she did, and we joked about having sympathetic pregnancy symptoms. When I returned home and shared the event with Pepe, I suddenly stopped mid-sentence. Curious, Pepe asked, "What's wrong?" I asked him to wait a minute and checked my cycle calendar. I realized I was nearly a month late. After taking three pregnancy tests, it was confirmed—I was pregnant.

Unfortunately, my relationship with Pepe hadn't improved; in fact, it had worsened. Soon after discovering my pregnancy, Pepe called me one night, Asking me to come over urgently. Fearing the worst about his father's health, who had been sick

with cancer, I rushed to his side. When I arrived, he confessed to being involved with another woman (who happened to be married) for most of our relationship. This revelation confirmed my earlier suspicions, I had shared with him about having a psychic vision about a brown-haired woman around him, which he dismissed and called me crazy. Although he didn't disclose how their relationship ended,

it involved lawyers and police, resulting in ongoing drama for a few months. Feeling trapped because I was already pregnant, I meditated on what to do, and internally, I felt compelled to stay.

Amid these revelations, my lease was up for renewal, and we decided that I would move in with Pepe and his parents to save money and eventually find a larger place together. As I navigated pregnancy, I contemplated when to take maternity leave. Working as an independent contractor without benefits, my disability insurance would only cover about a week. Trusting my dreams, I affirmed that I would dream of my son's date of birth. The next day, I woke up with a specific date in mind—June 24th, which was ten days before the doctor's estimated due date. Despite everyone's attempts to dissuade me, claiming I was crazy, I planned to take off a week before the date I dreamed about. However, I worked until two days before that date. On the 23rd, my water broke, but it was a slow leak, so I continued with my plans, including going to the independent theater to watch "The NeverEnding Story," which my son was named after. He was born the next day, on June 24th - the exact time I predicted.

After giving birth, I couldn't get my job back, and Pepe hadn't saved any money, leaving me solely responsible for all the bills and expenses related to the baby. Frustrated by the lack of income, support, and my own space, I ended up spending time with my mom, who provided immense help with the baby. During my stay, I explored job opportunities in the area, hoping to find something better than what I had. I received three job offers and informed Pepe that I planned to move to my mom's place, save money, and then we could live together once I had everything settled. Despite my mom living 2.5 hours away, I had grown more confident in trusting my intuition. When Pepe asked when I would move, I replied, "in two weeks." During that time, as I prepared to move, his father, ended up in critical condition and soon passed away around the time of my move. I understood the unfortunate timing, but I had to take action to survive and support my family. So, I continued with the move and discussed him coming after I found a place.

.

From New Beginnings to Heartbreak: Navigating Challenges and Discovering Transformation

When I lived with my mom, my relationship with Pepe continued deteriorating. It was a long-distance, on-and-off situation, but I remained determined to find a new place for myself and my child. It was during this period that the term "Twin Flames" entered my reality, leading me to delve deeper into my spiritual practices. Finally, when my son was about 1.5 years old, I managed to move into my place, which was a liberating feeling.

However, my newfound independence was short-lived. I received a call from my workplace informing me that I was being fired for supposedly competing with them. I had been working as an independent massage therapist and had been promoting myself at various events on my days off. Additionally, I recently took a cupping class and introduced the technique to the spa where I worked. Since it was a cutting-edge technique at the time, it gained popularity. The spa owner approached me, asking me to promote the spa during my events, but I requested compensation for my time and expenses. Unfortunately, they declined, claiming that I was competing with them. Suddenly, on my first day in my new place, I found myself without a job, with a 1-year-old to support. However, I reached out to a mentor who reminded me that this was the opportunity I had been asking for to start my own business. With newfound confidence, I managed to fill my schedule within a week and was fully booked for a month.

Regarding my relationship with Pepe, things took a different turn after I settled into my new place. Initially, he would visit every weekend to spend time with our son and, I thought, to spend time with me. We discussed the possibility of him moving in, but there always seemed to be some obstacle preventing it. In 2015, I found out I was pregnant for the second time. However, during this pregnancy, I started feeling increasingly distant from Pepe. I was constantly sick and experienced morning sickness throughout the entire pregnancy. Our communication dwindled, and when we did talk, it often led to arguments. I couldn't shake the feeling that something was being kept from me. Unfortunately, my concerns were dismissed as irrational and me being difficult.

During this pregnancy, I wanted to predict the birthdate, just like I had done before. One day, I woke up with a strong sense of when I would deliver. Two weeks before my expected due date from the doctor, I packed my bags and traveled 2.5 hours to Pepe's home. The reason was that I wanted the same midwife who had delivered my first child to be there for the birth of my second. On the first night at his place, I watched TV while he was at work. He called me after his shift, asking if I was hungry. We decided on what to eat and hung up. However, shortly after, the phone rang again.
"Hello?"

No one answered, but I could hear voices in the background. Naturally curious, I eavesdropped. I overheard Pepe complaining about me, how he had to help me move things, and how I was making him do so much. Then I heard a woman saying she was sorry he was going through that and how he was such a good guy for helping me. She professed her love for him and couldn't wait to spend more time with him.

My heart pounded in my chest. I asked my mother-in-law to watch my older son, got in my car, and left. As I pulled up to Pepe's workplace, I coincidentally arrived as the woman was leaving, just missing her. It became clear that he had been seeing another woman. To make a long story short, he had been living a separate life for the past two years. This woman did not know about my pregnancy until a few weeks before I came to his place to prepare for the arrival of our second son.

The stress of the situation caused intense cramping, leading me to be admitted to the hospital instead of giving birth at the birthing center as planned. Although I had to fight for four days to prevent them from attempting a C-section, thankfully everything turned out fine with the birth, having my second son on my predicted date. I had to stay with Pepe for about a week after the birth to heal, but as soon as I could, I left. I couldn't bear to be in the same house as him. I felt like his entire family hated me, and there were so many fabricated stories that I didn't know what to believe anymore.

Back in my own home with my two children, I spent the next six to eight months battling postpartum depression, dealing with a breakup, and experiencing what I now recognize as the dark night of the soul. The days were excruciatingly difficult, and I threw myself into work, keeping busy to avoid drowning in my thoughts. But when I put my kids to sleep, and it was just me and my thoughts, I felt overwhelmed. I would lay with my two boys around me, and once they were asleep, I would crawl out of bed and cry uncontrollably and frequently.

In the Depths of Despair

One day, as I found myself retreating to a corner to cry again, something within me said no. I had reached my breaking point. I no longer wanted to endure this kind of existence. I yearned for something different. It was then that my intuition guided me to my collection of aromatherapy oils, and I instinctively reached for Spikenard.

My mother described its scent as reminiscent of feet, and initially, I agreed with her assessment. So, I wasn't particularly thrilled when I uncapped the bottle and took a deep inhale. However, as the aroma filled my senses, I was pleasantly surprised. It carried a sweet and earthy quality that instantly calmed me and settled my mind.

Upon researching the properties of Spikenard, I couldn't help but laugh. Its sweet, woody root aroma has the potential to facilitate grounding and centering effects on the body and mind. It can aid in "cognitive flexibility," helping to reshape persistent thoughts of worry, anxiety, and repetitive thinking, thus allowing for the release of old wounds. My intuition had guided me perfectly.

For the next three months, I continued to wear and diffuse this aroma, finding solace in its effects. However, one day, as I went to apply it, I noticed that it now smelled like feet. It was then that I knew I no longer needed the Spikenard.

Amid my breakup with Pepe, he would often come over to my home to see the children. During these visits, he would manipulate me into believing that he wanted to leave the other woman and reunite our family. Initially, I attempted to keep us together and fix our relationship. However, deep down, I harbored anger and hatred towards him, and I didn't want him around. Each time he showed up, my body would immediately go into panic mode, and my anxiety would skyrocket. I found it impossible to remain calm in his presence. My body was overwhelmed with fury. It was during this turbulent time that I began exploring therapy options and stumbled upon EMDR therapy.

EMDR therapy, which stands for Eye Movement Desensitization and Reprocessing therapy, is a mental health treatment technique. It involves moving your eyes in a specific way while processing traumatic memories. The goal of EMDR is to help you heal from trauma or distressing life experiences. In a session, you can choose a specific trauma to work through and be guided by the therapist or allow your mind to take you wherever it needs to go.

I researched what EMDR therapy was about and booked a session, optimistic that it could help me with the anxiety I was experiencing. I had one session, and the next day, I was supposed to meet with Pepe and take the kids to the zoo. Surprisingly, EMDR therapy worked wonders. I spent the entire day with Pepe and the kids without an exaggerated negative response.

After this positive experience, I embarked on 30 days of no contact with Pepe. This time apart clarified my feelings about my tumultuous situation with him over the past seven years. As I moved forward, it became clear that I no longer desired to be with Pepe. I realized that I would much rather abandon the notion of "keeping my family together" out of fear of judgment from others. I prioritized my well-being and happiness above societal expectations.

Thrilled by the success of my first session, I decided to have a second one. During this second session, a significant childhood memory resurfaced: the first experience I had at the age of 4. In this memory, I was brought back to the room where my 5-year-old older brother and I were with our mom. She broke the news to us that our dad had died. My brother cried and blamed me for this tragedy. Our mother went to her room in tears, and our uncle was in the living room.

Meanwhile, I stood alone in the hallway, overwhelmed. It was at that moment that I first experienced abandonment. Feelings of guilt and shame surrounding my premonition arose within me. You see, I had dreamt of my father's death before it happened. So, the premonition became a painful reality when my father was murdered shortly after the dream. That event caused me to lose my father and deeply hurt the people I loved, along with my dreams.

This revelation during EMDR therapy was a significant turning point in my healing journey. With this newfound knowledge, I began unraveling many subconscious programs that were running in my mind, contributing to the chaos I had been experiencing in what I called my life—the repeating cycle of making negative choices over and
over again. I was ready to reclaim my life.

Love and Healing:
My Journey Towards Fulfilling Relationships

From sitting in corners, overwhelmed and in tears, to feeling empowered and in control of my emotions, I embarked on a journey of self-examination and self-accountability. I realized that no one was coming to save me, and I had two young children who depended on me. I was determined to initiate the change I so desperately desired.

Looking into my own eyes in the mirror, I began a voyage of self-discovery. It became apparent how deeply ingrained self-deprecating beliefs from past relationships, friends, and childhood experiences had affected me. Through my tears, I started the process of self-love by repeating the words, 'I love you' to myself. Gradually, I rekindled the love I had lost for myself. Each day marked progress as I gazed at my entire body in the mirror and sent it love.

My days were filled with intention. With no one to guide me, I learned to hold my own hand. The more I connected with myself and committed to my healing, the more my intuition expanded. I received inner guidance, from words to research to meditation techniques. I created space to quiet my mind, learning effective methods for my healing journey. I observed not only emotional transformations but physical ones as well, feeling free without the need to escape. I had found contentment.

As my self-love grew, I began to entertain the idea of meeting new people. Although I wasn't ready to date, I encountered the Shadow Man. I first learned about the shadow man from the psychic I met, went on a date with Pepe, almost 7 years prior. Neither I or the Shadow Man were looking for a relationship. We connected instantly, but my insecurities about men and relationships quickly resurfaced. Our meeting was through a group of friends; he suggested we all meet up for dinner and a movie. I was excited and nervous, which led me to drink – a vice I hadn't indulged in for five years. It was a wakeup call, and I knew I had to release it from my life once more.

Over the course of being with the Shadow Man, it has been an eye-opening and heartwarming healing journey. With a strong foundation in self-love, I began to explore what it meant to love another person. I continued using the methods I had mentioned earlier to address any lingering insecurities and beliefs about relationships and men that were holding me back from the fulfilling relationship I had always wanted. Like life itself, this journey is ongoing, and I'm grateful to have met someone equally dedicated to their self-exploration as I am to mine.

A Painful Realization

As I continued my healing journey and released the limitations of my mind, I realized that I no longer relate to most of the people I used to connect with. Despite this, I cherished my connections, but I mainly focused on my mission and kept to myself. However, I sometimes craved connection with others and wasn't always mindful of who I let into my life.

Being passionate about spirituality and helping others heal, I tended to overshare when someone was close to me. As I fully embraced my psychic gifts and lived aligned with my true self and life purpose, I had some heart-wrenching realizations about my relationships.

My cousin, the one from the house party, whom I considered my best friend, was again by my side. We grew closer after I broke up with Pepe, rekindling our best-friend bond. She even accompanied me to events where I promoted my business, helping with merchandise sales while I offered spiritual healing and readings. I trusted her completely, so when she expressed interest in starting her own psychic business, I wholeheartedly encouraged her.

Before my cousin embarked on her psychic business venture, she voiced concerns about people thinking she was copying me. I responded with a carefree "who gives a fuck what they think!" At the time, I didn't fully grasp the meaning behind her statement. However, everything became clear during an upcoming girls' trip.

Initially, I had reservations about going on the girls' trip due to work commitments. Eventually, I finished my tasks and packed up, driving to the hotel where we were staying. The trip included my cousin and her longtime friend, who had become somewhat of a friend to me. Although we didn't spend much time alone, we often hung out together. Unfortunately, my cousin's friend and I had clashed on several occasions.

During dinner one night, my cousin mentioned her successful social media following, prompting me to congratulate her on her remarkable achievement. I shared my struggles with growing my own social media presence and expressed admiration for her accomplishments in such a short time. Further into the night, Surprisingly, my friends attacked my business, criticizing my pricing as too high and accusing me of charging exorbitant amounts. I reminded them that I had been in the industry for over a decade, long before they entered, and that I believed my prices were fair given the value I provided.

Later, during a car ride to a local spiritual store, my cousin grew distant and began texting furiously. Curious, I asked her what she was doing and who she was talking to. She curtly replied, "I am working." I didn't understand her attitude, as I had merely commented on her excessive texting. Nevertheless, we arrived at the store, and I tried to lighten the mood by playfully dancing and rubbing against her. However, she snapped at me, accusing me of trying to steal her magic. I laughed it off, jokingly retorting that she was trying to take my energy. I moved on, entering a different room to continue shopping.

After purchasing my items, we all returned to the car to leave, and I noticed my cousin hadn't brought her things. When I asked her why, she said she returned them because of my comment about stealing her magic. Assuming she was joking, I laughed, but she was genuinely hurt and bothered by my words. Realizing my mistake, I immediately apologized and reassured her of my love, offering a hug. At that point, I thought we had resolved the issue, believing she had let it go.

As we ended the trip and began packing up, my cousin decided to ride home with me instead of our other friend. While loading our belongings into the car, I overheard our friend say to my cousin, "Well, hopefully, the car ride home isn't as bad." Although I couldn't comprehend the context of their conversation, it felt like my cousin was bad-mouthing me to our friend. Consumed with anger, I put on my headphones and remained silent for the entire ride home. The situation drained me, and I couldn't bear the negative energy from my cousin, who seemed abrasive and constantly spoke ill of me.

The next day, I woke up to messages from my cousin accusing me of unfollowing her on social media and suggesting that I needed to work on myself, projecting onto others. She claimed that I accused everyone else of needing healing work except for myself. In response, I clarified that I hadn't unfollowed her on social media since

I maintained separate business and personal accounts. I urged her to double-check because everything appeared the same on my end. Additionally, I confronted her about her behavior, to which she denied any wrongdoing.

Shortly after that, the beginning of the month arrived, and I sent out my monthly newsletter to my clients. Unfortunately, I realized my cousin was still on my email list when I discovered she had copied and shared my email verbatim. It was at that moment I realized there was a snake in my yard. Not only had she been posting similar readings to mine, but at lower prices, she was now copying my marketing strategies. Furious, I blocked her from accessing my business account. Later on, our mutual friend reached out to me, and when I informed her that I had blocked my cousin, she accused me of constantly fighting and causing problems with my cousin before blocking me herself. I was shocked because I had never been in a fight with my cousin.

This revelation made me realize that I had been blind to all the times my cousin had lied to me and spoken ill of me, inventing stories about me to her birthday party guests and friends and who knows who else. It suddenly made sense why she would talk poorly about everyone else to me—she was likely doing the same behind my back.

For months, I questioned my intuition, contemplating how I could have been so blind to someone so close to me taking advantage of my knowledge and acting deceitfully towards me. These thoughts plagued my mind, causing me to doubt my psychic gifts and judgment. I continuously rambled, replaying my cousin's actions and internalizing their impact on me.

However, this introspection led me to an important realization in my healing journey. I had to accept that some people aren't conscious of the things they do because they haven't done the inner work. The rightful thing I can do for myself is recognize this and have compassion for these souls, especially since I have once been in their shoes. Their behavior has nothing to do with my worth or capabilities. This breakthrough freed me from the burden of self-blame and allowed me to shift my focus towards personal growth and serving others.

Unfortunately, when you change and begin to radiate your light, you may face attacks from those around you who haven't found their inner light. They may be irritated by your growth because they haven't achieved it themselves. To this I say, keep going. The right people will find you.

Lessons Learned and Moving Forward

As I reflect on my journey, it's essential to acknowledge that my life and childhood weren't solely defined by trauma and unhappiness. I believe in the inherent goodness of most people, often veiled by their unresolved wounds and a lack of communication skills. I've learned to look beyond the projections and see the wounded child within, yearning for acceptance and validation. Embracing this perspective, I've balanced my recognition of perfection in everything and everyone with the need for discernment and maintaining healthy boundaries.

During my time with Iago, I acquired profound lessons in discipline and hard work. The world of entrepreneurship opened its doors to me, and I gained a new level of confidence in the business arena, igniting my passion for personal ventures. I transitioned from a life of struggle to one of comfort, instilling in me the profound value of tenacity and determination. Living on the farm exposed me to a holistic lifestyle, emphasizing the significance of food choices, even if it included animal-based products. I cultivated the ability to differentiate between food produced by major corporations and that sourced from small farms. Beyond these lessons, I acquired invaluable life skills.

Through it all, my mother remained a constant source of support. Her unwavering presence in my life proved that, regardless of any manipulation, her love and support were unwavering. The truth is, my mother was as much a victim of Iago as I was. We were all victims of the circumstances we found ourselves in.

The stories I've shared represent some of the most powerful

experiences that kept me trapped in a negative cycle, yearning for an escape. Writing this book itself unearthed more negative memories and experiences. Shadow work is a complex journey, but as you learn to look at it from an outsider's perspective, it becomes easier to shed those heavy emotional burdens and move forward. As you embark on your healing journey, remember to be mindful of where you invest your energy. Self-work won't change the people around you or render you immune to life's challenges, but it will empower you to navigate them with confidence. Always remember, you have the ability to shape your own path.

This journey is an ongoing, ever-evolving process. Just when we think we've worked through it all, new layers can emerge. Forgiveness, especially self-forgiveness, is a vital part of this voyage. Approach it with gentleness and compassion as you traverse the path of healing.

The Meaning Behind Changed Names

In the vast tapestry of stories, names hold a special significance, and in this section, we delve into the meaning behind the changed names that grace the previous pages.

Iago

Derived from the fictional character in Shakespeare's "Othello," Iago embodies the main antagonist who manipulates and schemes against Othello. Described as a Machiavellian figure, Iago is renowned for his deceitful nature and his ability to maintain a facade of honesty while plotting the downfall of those around him.

Yunho

Inspired by Yunho Kim, a character from the Korean drama "Rooftop Prince," Yunho is portrayed as a laid-back drummer with a relaxed personality.

Caligula

Evoking the notorious Roman emperor, Caligula, this name carries the weight of reckless behavior, extreme extravagance, and sexual excess.

Huck

Taken from the beloved character Huckleberry Finn, created by Mark Twain, Huck represents a spirit of adventure, freedom, and rebellion against societal constraints. Huck Finn's character is known for his wit, resourcefulness, and his journey towards self-discovery along the Mississippi River.

Earnest

An homage to Ernest Hemingway, the renowned American writer, the name Earnest carries with it the complexities of emotional intelligence and a tumultuous personal life. Hemingway's love for fishing and his literary prowess lend depth to this character, imbuing them with a mix of passion and struggles.

Pepe

Inspired by Pepe le Pew, the iconic skunk from Looney Tunes, this name brings a touch of whimsy and charm. Pepe le Pew is known for his relentless pursuit of love, often with comical and misguided results.

Catherine de Medici

Drawing from the historical figure of Catherine de Medici, the name represents a woman of political cunning, social finesse, and involvement in intrigues. While known for her manipulative actions, Catherine de Medici was also regarded as a polite and charming figure, showcasing her multifaceted nature.

"The secret of change is to focus all your energy not on fighting the old, but on building the new."

Socrates

Chapter 3
Cultivating Self Love

Defining Self Love

Learning to Love Yourself

"Self-love is a devotion
to yourself
through embracing your
authenticity."

Shannon aka The Spiritual Gangsta

Defining Self Love

For years, I wandered through life, convinced that I had mastered the art of self-love. Little did I know, I was merely treading water in a vast ocean of self-deception, completely oblivious to the truth. It wasn't until I mustered the courage to confront my innermost self that I realized the shocking revelation—I had been living a facade, and my understanding of self-love was nothing more than a hazy mirage.

Perhaps you can relate. When I first embarked on this journey of self-love, I found myself lost in a labyrinth of confusion. What did it truly mean to love oneself? What did it look like, or even feel like? Doubts crept into my mind, and I often found myself second-guessing my every move, questioning if I was truly embracing this elusive concept in the right way.

self-love

noun

1. regard for one's own well-being and happiness (chiefly considered as a desirable rather than narcissistic characteristic).

The definition of self-love refers to the regard and care one has for their own well-being, happiness, and overall worth. It encompasses a deep appreciation and acceptance of oneself, including one's strengths, weaknesses, and unique qualities. Self-love involves treating oneself with kindness, compassion, and respect, and prioritizing personal growth and fulfillment.

At its core, self-love involves recognizing one's inherent value and deservingness of love, without the need for external validation. It means acknowledging and nurturing one's physical, emotional, mental, and spiritual needs, and engaging in practices that promote self-care and self-compassion. Self-love also encompasses setting healthy boundaries and honoring one's own values, beliefs, and desires. It involves embracing authenticity and living in alignment with one's true self, rather than conforming to external expectations or seeking approval from others.

Practicing self-love involves cultivating a positive and. supportive inner dialogue, challenging self-critical thoughts, and replacing them with self-affirming beliefs. It includes celebrating one's achievements, no matter how small, and recognizing personal growth and progress. Self-love is an ongoing process of self-discovery, self-acceptance, and self-care. It requires consistent self-reflection, self-awareness, and a commitment to nurturing a healthy and loving relationship with oneself.

However, self-love can sometimes be mistaken for confidence, especially after a significant life event such as a breakup. Picture this: after a heart-wrenching breakup, a newfound surge of confidence seems to bubble up from within. It's a false dawn, a mirage of self-assuredness that can be deceiving. For a while, it feels like conquering the world, fueled by a desire to prove one's worth and desirability. Yet, upon closer examination, it becomes evident that this newfound confidence is not rooted in genuine self-love or self-acceptance.

It's a defense mechanism, an overcompensation for the emotional wounds left by the breakup. It's the mind's way of shielding itself from the pain and rejection, projecting an image of strength to the outside world. However, this pseudo-confidence is fragile, easily shattered by a word or a thought that brushes against the unresolved emotions lurking beneath the surface. True self-love is not a reactionary response to external events; it's a deep, abiding relationship with oneself that remains steadfast through life's highs and lows.

As we navigate the journey of self-love, it's essential to distinguish between these moments of fleeting confidence and the enduring embrace of authentic self-love. Recognizing this difference allows us to embark on a genuine journey toward self-discovery, acknowledging our wounds, healing them, and truly cultivating a foundation of love and acceptance within ourselves. It's a process that takes time, patience, and a willingness to face our innermost fears and insecurities.

We will journey deeper into the realm of self-love, we unveil the facades and the fleeting illusions of confidence. We arrive at the core question: how do we authentically love ourselves? The answer is not in a singular act or a prescribed routine but in the conscious cultivation of love, care, and acceptance for the most important person in our lives—ourselves.

"Everyone says to
Love yourself,
but no one is telling us how."

Shannon aka The Spiritual Gangsta

Learning to Love Yourself

The enigma of self-love haunted my thoughts for what felt like an eternity, as I grappled with the question: How do we truly love ourselves? It seemed as though the answers were always vague clichés, leaving me skeptical and yearning for a more profound understanding. A simple act like taking a long bath, they said, would unlock the gates of self-love. But was it that simplistic? I found myself submerged in these waters of contemplation, seeking the elusive truth.

The paradox emerged—I realized that self-love encompassed more than a singular act or a prescribed ritual. It was a dance of presence, an intimate connection with oneself that infused intention into every moment. It was the art of being fully engaged in the present, infusing our actions with purpose and authenticity.

Imagine setting up a spiritual bath—the very act becomes a sacred expression of self-love. It begins with the deliberate selection of herbs and oils, handpicked to infuse the water with nourishing energies. The ambiance you create wraps you in a cocoon of tranquility, harmonizing with your inner essence. You offer prayers to the universe, infusing the water with your intentions.

And as you sink into the tub, the words you speak to yourself become a symphony of self-affirmation, serenading your soul with love and acceptance.

Self-love extends far beyond the confines of a bath. It permeates every facet of our existence, inviting us to engage consciously with ourselves. It is in the act of savoring a delicious meal, relishing each bite as an expression of self-nourishment. It is in the moments of solitude, as we immerse ourselves in a captivating book that ignites our passions and expands our horizons. It is in the awareness of the breeze blowing across your face as it gently reminds you of your strength and resilience. And it is in the conversations we have with ourselves, showering our minds with empowering affirmations and banishing self-doubt to the shadows.

In matters of self-love, there is no singular path to follow. It is a symphony of mindful moments, intentional acts, and deep self-connection. It is the embrace of authenticity, the celebration of our unique journey. So, as you embark upon this voyage of self-love, weave intention into every moment of your existence. With each conscious choice, with each present moment, you cultivate the seeds of self-worth and spark the flames of love within. So,yes, sometimes selflove may look like taking a bath as long as the intention is there.

In the upcoming chapters, we will explore the practical and profound ways to manifest self-love. From nurturing your inner dialogue to embracing your unique journey, from setting empowering boundaries to fostering a deep sense of gratitude, we will embark on a guided expedition into the heart of self-love. exploring the intricacies of self-love, the patterns that influence our perspectives, and the transformative practices that guide us towards a genuine and lasting sense of love for ourselves. It's about discovering the art of being kind to yourself, of honoring your essence, and of nurturing the seeds of love that resides within. Together, we'll unravel the complexities of the heart and mind, and step into the realm of true self-love—an unshakable foundation upon which we can build a vibrant and authentic future.

Some examples of ways to practice Self-Love

Take a Spiritual Bath

Spend Time Alone

Journal

Read a Book

Say No When Overwhelmed

Do A Beauty Routine

Make a Special Meal

Meditate

Exercise

Write a Letter

Go Spend Time in Nature

_____

_____

_____

An intention is a guiding principle for how you want to show up in the world, a statement of purpose that you want to align yourself with.

Intentions come from the heart and are driven by a desire to connect with our authentic selves.

Unknown

Chapter 4
Exploring Inner Patterns

Unveiling the Power of Triggers

10 Common Trigger Categories

Why Perspective Matters

"Holding onto anger is like drinking poison and expecting the other person to die"

Buddha

Unveiling the Power of Triggers

Triggers, in the context of emotions and mental well-being, refer to stimuli or events that elicit a strong emotional or psychological response in an individual. These triggers can vary greatly from person to person and can be associated with past experiences, traumatic events, or deeply ingrained beliefs.

Triggers can take various forms, including sights, sounds, smells, physical sensations, specific words or phrases, or even certain social situations. When exposed to a trigger, an individual may experience intense emotional reactions such as fear, anger, sadness, anxiety, or a sense of unease. Triggers have the power to evoke memories or associations tied to past events or traumas, causing the person to relive or re-experience the emotions and distress associated with those experiences.

Understanding personal triggers can be influential in managing and coping with the associated emotional responses. Through therapy, self-reflection, and various coping strategies, individuals can learn to identify triggers, develop effective techniques to manage their emotional reactions, and work towards healing to reduce the impact of triggers on their overall well-being.

Recognizing triggers is a critical step in managing your emotional responses and engaging in shadow work. Sometimes the signs are easy to detect and sometimes they are subtle enough for us to easily overlook them. Here are some ways to help you recognize when you're triggered:

Emotional Reaction:

Sudden and Strong Emotions: An overwhelming surge of emotions (anger, fear, sadness) that seems disproportionate to the current situation.

Rapid Mood Shifts: Going from feeling fine to feeling extremely upset, anxious, or angry within a short period.

Physical Sensations:

Increased Heart Rate: Feeling your heart racing or palpitations.

Shallow Breathing or Hyperventilation: Rapid or shallow breathing, a feeling of breathlessness, or even a sensation of suffocation.

Muscle Tension: Feeling your muscles tense, especially in the neck, shoulders, or jaw.

Sweating: Sudden onset of sweating, even if the environment isn't particularly warm.

Cognitive Responses:

Rumination: Dwelling on a particular thought, scenario, or memory that is distressing.

Intrusive Thoughts: Thoughts that seem to invade your mind and are difficult to control or push away.

Difficulty Concentrating: Struggling to focus or concentrate on tasks due to the intensity of your emotions.

Behavioral Signs:

Fight or Flight Response: Reacting impulsively or aggressively (fight) or feeling a strong urge to escape or avoid the situation (flight).

Avoidance: Purposefully steering clear of certain people, places, or situations to prevent a potential trigger.

10 Common Trigger Categories

Exploring Emotional Responses of Triggers

For the sake of this book we are going to focus on triggers that would require shadow work. Shadow work is a psychological and introspective process aimed at exploring and integrating the unconscious or "shadow" aspects of one's personality. These aspects are often hidden, repressed, or denied, and they can be triggered by certain situations or experiences. Shadow work helps individuals confront these triggers and work through the underlying issues. Here are some examples of triggers that may require someone to do shadow work:

Rejection and Abandonment:

Feeling intense emotions of fear or unworthiness when faced with rejection, abandonment, or perceived neglect. Shadow work may help explore past experiences that contributed to these feelings and address any unresolved issues related to attachment and self-worth.

Criticism and Judgement:

Reacting strongly to criticism or feeling judged by others, which may stem from unresolved self-esteem issues or childhood experiences where one's actions or behaviors were constantly criticized or judged.

Control and Power:

Feeling triggered by situations where one perceives a lack of control or experiences power struggles. Exploring these triggers may reveal deeper issues related to autonomy, trust, or past experiences of powerlessness.

Intimacy and Vulnerability:

Struggling to open up or be vulnerable in intimate relationships due to past experiences of betrayal, emotional hurt, or a fear of being emotionally exposed.

Jealousy and Envy:

Feeling overwhelmed by jealousy or envy towards others, which may indicate unresolved feelings of inadequacy or unmet desires.

Anger and Aggression:

Reacting with intense anger or aggression in certain situations, possibly rooted in past trauma, unexpressed emotions, or unresolved conflicts.

Abuse and Trauma:

Experiencing emotional flashbacks or intense emotions when confronted with situations reminiscent of past abuse or trauma. Shadow work can help process and heal these traumatic experiences.

Repeating Patterns:

Noticing recurring patterns in relationships or behaviors that lead to negative outcomes, which may indicate unresolved issues that need to be addressed.

Avoidance:

Feeling compelled to avoid certain situations, emotions, or topics because they trigger discomfort or anxiety. Shadow work can explore the underlying reasons for these avoidance mechanisms.

Self-Sabotage:

Engaging in self-destructive behaviors or patterns that hinder personal growth and success. Shadow work can help uncover the root causes of self-sabotage and work towards self-compassion and self-improvement.

Trigger Transformation Method

When it comes to triggers, our goal is not just to identify them; we must actively work to resolve their hold on us. Merely recognizing triggers is insufficient—true healing occurs when we unravel their emotional grasp on our psyche. Many find it challenging to navigate this emotional labyrinth and release these triggers. Over time, I've come to perceive the world as an expansive mirror reflecting our beliefs and self-perceptions. Building upon this realization, I've developed the Trigger Transformation Method (TTM), a potent approach to heal triggers by delving deep into the core of these issues for a thorough resolution. Let me guide you through this transformative journey.

Trigger Transformation Method (TTM):

The Trigger Transformation Method is a powerful tool for identifying and healing triggers. Here's an example of how to use this method:

1. **Identify the Trigger:** Begin by recognizing the trigger and the associated emotion. For instance, imagine a scenario where a cashier at a grocery store ignores your greeting, leading to irritation throughout the day. Write down: *"I'm irritated with the cashier for ignoring me."*

2. **Reframe Towards Yourself:** Rewrite the trigger statement, directing it towards yourself. In this case, it becomes: *"I'm upset with myself because I've been ignoring myself."*

3. **Assess Truthfulness:** Ask yourself if this statement holds truth for you. Initially, it may seem perplexing, but upon reflection, you might realize that you've been neglecting your own needs and desires. Validate this by acknowledging the truth.

4. **Honor and Resolution:** Next, explore ways to honor yourself in this situation and release the emotion. In this case, recognizing your exhaustion, you decide that taking a 30-minute nap would be a way to honor your needs and regain a sense of well-being.

Trigger Transformation Method (TTM): Navigating a Serious Trigger

The Trigger Transformation Method can be an invaluable tool for dealing with more serious triggers, such as experiences of abuse. Here's an example of how to use this method:

1. **Identify the Trigger:** Start by acknowledging the specific trigger and the emotions tied to it. For instance, let's consider a scenario where past abuse experiences have left emotional scars. Write down: "*I feel immense fear and anxiety when recalling past abuse experiences.*"

2. **Reframe Towards Yourself:** Reformulate the trigger statement, focusing it towards yourself. In this case, it transforms to: "*I'm struggling to heal and find peace within myself after enduring past abuse.*"

3. **Assess Truthfulness:** This part can take some time to work through because whenever we are at the negative end of a situation, we don't want to put the blame onto us, but if you are able to acknowledge the deep-rooted impact of abuse, you could come to find you have continued to treat yourself poorly because of a negative neural pathway created from a result of the situation. Acknowledgment of this allows you to take steps towards clearing it. Reflect on the statement and inquire if this resonates with your experience.

Continue to reflect and validate the truth in this reframed statement.

4. **Honor and Resolution:** Explore ways to honor yourself and seek resolution. This could involve seeking therapy, joining support groups, or confiding in a trusted individual. It's about acknowledging your pain and taking constructive steps towards healing.

By utilizing the Trigger Transformation Method (TTM) in the context of a serious trigger like abuse, you're not trivializing the trauma but providing a framework to confront and address it. Recognizing the truth, honoring your feelings, and seeking appropriate help are vital steps towards healing and growth.

"We drink the poison our minds pour for us and wonder why we feel so sick"

Atticus

The Power of Perception

Perspective is a powerful lens through which we perceive and interpret the world, including ourselves. How we view ourselves, whether it stems from childhood experiences or more recent events, often becomes distorted due to the repetition of negative remarks and internalizing the words of others. This distorted self-perception manifests when we look in the mirror and engage in negative self-talk, which not only diminishes our sense of self-worth and confidence, but also impacts our overall energy and well-being.

Some may feel perspective can not simply change because of the facts of how a past situation played out, however, perception is within our control to change. Perception is not about the facts of a situation, but how we fell about a situation. Either the glass is half full or half empty. Either you have something to drink or someone only served you half a glass. We have the ability to change this damaging behavior going on inside our minds and heal any distortions we have about our lives and self-image. We can release the lower vibrational frequencies, negative thoughts, and emotions that have weighed us down. As we heal our perspective we cultivate self-compassion and replace self-deprecating thoughts with empowering ones. By nurturing a positive perspective, we uplift our vibration, promote a sense of ease within ourselves, and amplify positive energy. As our self-perception improves, our confidence naturally rises, empowering us to navigate our experiences with greater self-assurance. We become open to more pleasant and fulfilling as our newfound positive energy and self-belief attract positive opportunities and relationships. By shifting our perspective and embracing a healthier self-image, we unlock the potential for greater happiness, personal growth, and overall well-being.

Remember, perspective matters. It shapes our reality and influences how we interact with ourselves and the world around us. By consciously choosing a perspective rooted in self-acceptance, love, and positivity, we can transform our lives and create a more fulfilling and joyful existence.

When you heal your perception of yourself, you gain:

Increased love for self & others

Confidence to pursue your dreams/desires

Increased Self-worth

Less Judgment

Trust in yourself & others

Better Boundaries

THE MIND

Chapter 5
Rewiring the Mind

Subconscious Mind

Neural Pathways

"Until you make the unconscious conscious, it will direct your life and you will call it fate."

C.G. JUNG

The Subconscious Mind

How do you feel about your life? Do you feel its easy or do you feel you are fated to have a trial-some life? What are the daily thoughts you have, do you even know? Queen's University researchers discovered we have more than 6,000 thoughts each day and some researchers say we can have upwords of 12,000 thoughts. Most of these thoughts are happening in the Subconscious mind. So how many of those 6,000 to 12,000 thoughts do you feel you are actually fully aware and conscious about having?

What is the subconscious mind? The subconscious mind refers to a part of our mind that operates below the level of conscious awareness. It includes thoughts, beliefs, memories, and emotions that are not currently in our conscious awareness but still influence our thoughts, behaviors, and feelings. The subconscious mind plays a significant role in shaping our perceptions, habits, and responses to various situations. It is responsible for automatic and instinctive behaviors, such as driving a car or riding a bicycle, which we do without consciously thinking about the individual actions involved and most people arent aware of it at all. Since most of what you think is something programmed from your childhood into your subconscious mind these subconscious, also called unconscious thoughts, naturally can cause unwanted triggers, much like the triggers we spoke about earlier. Unfortunately, the subconcious mind is the driving force behind the mass majority of peoples lives.

Let's step into the shoes of an average American and unravel their day, strongly influenced by what's brewing beneath the surface—the subconscious mind. Picture the sun peeking through the curtains, signaling the start of the day. They follow their usual morning routine, but as their mind stirs, it's not all sunshine. Negative thoughts creep in about their job, their appearance—doubts that cloud the morning.

Next up, their trusty smartphone steals the spotlight, an immediate dive into the digital world. However, today's news is far from uplifting. Stories of soaring housing prices, rising inflation, and crime flood their screen, painting the world in a shade of uncertainty. It's a shaky start to the day.

Lunchtime arrives amidst a chorus of complaints from co-workers—health issues and the strains of challenging relationships are the theme. They realize they haven't packed lunch, so the plan goes awry, opting for the quick fix—eating out.

Evening descends, and the craving for an escape grows stronger. The TV offers a portal to mind-numbing shows, a break from the dissonance of the day. Their phone becomes a refuge too, a scroll through social media perhaps, a way to distract from the noise of reality.

A drink in hand might seem inviting, a temporary solace.

Dinner is the next act, and they opt for the easy choice—a meal out, no fuss. The night deepens, and in the stillness of their room, the phone becomes a companion once more, the screen a gentle glow in the dim room. More scrolling—a way to delay the inevitable call of sleep.

In this ordinary day, the subconscious mind has taken the lead role, subtly influencing every scene. A life like this soon leads one to having a "mid-life crisis," which the American people have been led to believe is a normal occurrence in ones life time. Yet, awareness is the key. Recognizing these subtle whispers, or opertunities for awareness, would allow them to rewrite the script, to seek a new melody that resonates with their true desires. Becoming aware or conscious about one's actions and thoughts can orchestrate a conscious and authentic life, creating a tune that sings to their heart's desires and dreams.

"Conscious living helps you to think first and act second."

Jey Shetty

Neural Pathways

Neural pathways are the connections formed by networks of neurons in the brain. These pathways are responsible for transmitting information and facilitating communication between different areas of the brain. They allow electrical signals and chemical neurotransmitters to travel and exchange information, enabling various cognitive and physical functions.

Neural pathways are created through a process called neuroplasticity, which refers to the brain's ability to reorganize itself by forming new connections and strengthening existing ones. This process occurs throughout our lives as a response to learning, experiences, and environmental stimuli.

When it comes to the subconscious mind, neural pathways play a crucial role. As we repeatedly think certain thoughts or engage in particular behaviors, neural pathways associated with those thoughts or behaviors become stronger and more efficient. This process is often referred to as "neurons that fire together wire together."

For example, if you consistently think positive thoughts, you are reinforcing positive neural pathways in your subconscious mind. Conversely, if you frequently dwell on negative thoughts, you strengthen negative neural pathways. Over time, these reinforced pathways can influence your automatic thought patterns, emotional responses, and behavioral tendencies, the things you think, the things you eat, even the people you hang with.

Understanding the relationship between the subconscious mind and neural pathways can be valuable in personal development and change. Since we know we can strengthen and weaken neural pathways this means we can intentionally change our brain simply by intentionally focusing on positive thoughts and behaviors. This is how you can work towards rewiring your subconscious mind and creating new, more empowering neural pathways. When we make changes to our current behaviors, our brain adapts to these changes rewiring or connecting existing neurons in new ways, adding different connections while strengthening existing neural pathways. The brain then removes the old wired behaviors from the subconscious mind and replaces it with the new desired pathway.

Let's consider some examples of neural pathways involving self-esteem and self-doubt:

Negative Neural Pathway: The Self-Doubt Loop

Imagine you've been wanting to start a new fitness routine. You decide to go to a gym, but as you walk in, you start feeling anxious. Negative thoughts flood your mind: "I'm not fit enough for this. I'll never be able to keep up. People will judge me." These thoughts activate a well-worn neural pathway associated with self-doubt.

Negative Neural Pathway Reinforcement

Every time you enter the gym, these negative thoughts strengthen the neural connections. Over time, this loop becomes automatic. You start avoiding the gym, perpetuating the negative pathway and reinforcing the belief that you can't succeed.

Positive Neural Pathway: The Empowerment Loop

Now, let's imagine a different scenario. You enter the gym and instead focus on positive thoughts: "I'm taking a step towards a healthier me. Everyone starts somewhere. I can do this." These positive thoughts initiate a new neural pathway associated with self-empowerment.

Positive Neural Pathway Reinforcement

As you continue this positive self-talk and take action, these thoughts strengthen the neural connections associated with empowerment. You feel more confident, and as you progress in your fitness journey, the pathway becomes reinforced, influencing your belief in yourself and fostering further positive actions.

The Self-Doubt Loop

When we are in the negative Neural Pathway the effect causes anxiety, avoidance, low self-esteem, and missed opportunities for growth. Consequently hindering personal growth, creating a negative impact on mental and physical well-being through missed life experiences.

The Empowerment Loop

On the opposite side when we create a positive Neural Pathway the effect can create confidence, action-taking, improved self-esteem, and personal growth. Consequently allowing enhanced mental and physical well-being with opportunities for growth through fulfilling experiences.

This is why becoming conscious of your thoughts and changing your dialog is a vital part in changing your life. If you want have a different life you have to start with changing the inner thoughts.

In conclusion it's essential to underscore the profound impact our inner dialogue has on our lives. The thoughts we harbor, the conversations we have with ourselves, shape the lens through which we perceive the world and ourselves within it. If we aspire to lead a different, more enriched life, the transformation must initiate from within. Your inner world determines your outer reality, and this starts with nurturing empowering thoughts and fostering a positive, self-affirming dialogue.

As we transition to the next chapter, we delve deeper into a practice we refer to as 'Reflection Healing.' This practice is an introspective journey that focuses on how we perceive and speak to ourselves, particularly in the sacred space of the mirror. It's a journey towards self-love, self-acceptance, and empowerment. By consciously engaging with our own reflection, we open a gateway to healing, growth, and self-discovery.

Join me in exploring the transformative power of reflecting upon oneself, developing a deeper connection to yourself, and unlocking the potential to nurture a profound sense of self. Through 'Reflection Healing,' we set the stage for a beautiful metamorphosis within, one that radiates outward and touches every aspect of our lives.

Chapter 6
Connecting Deeper

Unveiling The Self

Rewriting Your Story through Reflection Healing

How to do Reflection Healing

Potential Encounters During Reflection Healing

7 week fast track Reflection Healing Schedule

"I am a big believer in the mirror test. All that matters is if you can look in the mirror and honestly tell the person you see there, that you've done your best."

John McKay

Connecting Deeper

What I will be sharing with you in this chapter is, by far, one of the most empowering practices I did along my journey. I never knew how disconnected I was to my true self until I attempted this exercise and as I share this exercise with others, I see them experience the same feelings and impact it had on me, and now. I am going to share it with you. This profound practice is what I call 'Reflection Healing.' Just as we've previously acknowledged the significance of reshaping our thoughts and nurturing empowering neural pathways, we now turn our focus towards our reflection—the symbolic gateway to our true selves.

On the path to healing, we must release the burdens of our past. Carrying the weight of previous experiences only anchors us to their conditions. Releasing the past acts as a bridge, connecting who we were to who we are becoming. It's a moment of letting go and healing, shedding the heaviness of our past to embrace a future illuminated by endless possibilities.

Imagine your emotional baggage as a heavy backpack you've been carrying for far too long. It's filled with past hurts, regrets, and negative emotions that have silently tethered you to a time that no longer serves you. Releasing energy is about unzipping that backpack and carefully removing each item, feeling the weight lift as you let go.

The quote, "The eyes are the window to the Soul," comes to mind when I think of this practice. I began this because I wanted to connect to me, my Soul, my Inner Self. Don't get me wrong, the reason I started this wasn't because I loved myself, and, if anything, this proved to me how much I didn't like myself at all. I remember walking up to the mirror in absolute anger and defeat and asking What. The. Fuck! No, I was confronting myself and saying, wtf was I here for, and why did I have such a shitty life. Why was I dealing with all these negative experiences? I was 36-37 years old. I should have this life thing figured out by now, and everyone but me seemed to have it figured out. Instead, I stood in front of the mirror at my very lowest.

I had one of those long mirrors that went across the whole bathroom wall, and out of exhaustion, I sat backward on the toilet. Still looking in the mirror, between crying fits, I took a deep breath and began to look deep into my eyes. That's when everything shifted. I was fed up and wanted different. I wanted answers.

At first, I just sat there. The silence was comforting. Yet who was I looking at? The longer I looked, the less the silence was there. I started to hear an internal dialog, and it wasn't pleasant. The things on repeat weren't even my thoughts; they were things others had said to me.

As I continued to sit there, becoming aware, my subconscious mind was now conscious. I could hear the negative programming going on, and with that knowledge, I could change it. After a few tries, I got the voices to shut up and was then able to rewrite the stories, starting with three simple words, "I Love You."

As we stand at this part of our transformative journey, we introduce 'Reflection Healing.' This practice invites you to gaze into the mirror not merely to observe your physical self but to delve deeper into your inner being—the thoughts, emotions, and beliefs that define you. The mirror becomes a sacred space—a portal to the essence of who you are. It's a reflective surface that mirrors not just your physical form but your soul's journey, your inner dialogues, and the stories etched within you. By engaging consciously with your reflection, you open the doors to profound self-awareness and healing.

"For our improvement we need a mirror."

Arthur Schopenhauer

Rewriting Your Story

Reflection Healing is an invitation to reclaim the narrative of your life. It's a journey of self-compassion, self-acceptance, and self-love. It's about acknowledging and honoring the person you see in the mirror, unconditionally and authentically.

On the following pages we'll embark on a guided journey, where you'll engage with your reflection in deliberate and transformative ways. Each week, you'll have the opportunity to explore different aspects of the self, gently peeling back layers, and revealing the beauty and strength within.

Through this practice, you'll learn to rewrite your story. You'll infuse it with love, kindness, and empowerment. You'll free yourself from the shackles of self-doubt and negative self-perception, emerging as a beacon of self-love and a harbinger of change.

So, prepare yourself to step into the realm of 'Reflection Healing.' Let the mirror become a metaphorical looking glass into your soul, a path to unburdening, healing, and ultimately, a journey towards self-love.

How to do Reflection Healing

Not much is needed to start with Reflection Healing; all you need is yourself, a mirror large enough to see both your eyes and a lot of courage. Some will find this easy, and others may find this to be the hardest thing in the book. Either way, I encourage you to continue until you, without a doubt, know you have mastered this.

To start, you will be looking into your eyes for 1 minute without saying anything. As you look into your eyes, make a note of any thoughts that come up, but do not become consumed by the thoughts. Repeat this for the first week.

The second week you will continue to look into your eyes for 1 minute, but this time you will be saying, "I love you" aloud or to yourself. Don't be alarmed if this brings up some emotion. If there is any emotion allow it to flow and continue to repeat, "I love you."

After the second week, increase the time from 1 minute to 2 minutes. Each week your goal is to increase the time you look in the mirror, getting up to 5 minutes while saying, "I love you," and any other affirmations that resonate with you. All without an emotional pull.

Potential Encounters during Reflection Healing

It's important to note that during this process, various emotions and triggers may surface. This is actually a positive sign, as it means you're exposing the subconscious thoughts that are running through your mind. Let's delve into the potential experiences you may encounter during this journey and discuss how to effectively navigate them.

Difficulty in Focus: A common challenge you might face is an influx of thoughts, making it difficult to connect with yourself during the Reflection Healing. Finding a quiet space is crucial for this practice. If you find your mind racing while looking in the mirror, grab a piece of paper and jot down these thoughts. Avoid analyzing or revisiting them. Simply write. Once done, return to the mirror, set a timer, and aim for a clear mind. You can dispose of the paper or even burn it—just exercise caution!

Emotional Responses: Congratulations, you're experiencing emotions! It's essential to be gentle with yourself. In my initial week of practicing this, tears were my constant companion. It's important to acknowledge and allow these emotions to flow freely. Avoid the urge to analyze or criticize them in the moment. Let them wash over you, and once they subside, you'll gain clarity on whether they require further exploration.

Trigger Management: If you encounter a trigger during the exercise, it's crucial to address and release it before proceeding. However, don't let it become an excuse to avoid Reflection Healing. I recommend addressing the trigger using the TTM in chapter 4. Once addressed, return to the Reflection Healing exercise.

"Be greatful for triggers,
they show you where you are
not free."

Unknown

Reflection Healing Exercise

On the following page, you'll find a suggested 7-week fast track to Reflection Healing. However, it's essential to remember that this is merely a proposed outline. Allow yourself the time you need to release and maintain the energy of each week.

This is a journey, not a race. Rushing through these exercises may result in spiritual bypassing and deprive you of the best possible outcome. Conversely, if you feel good and are tempted to shorten the exercise duration, I encourage you to resist the urge. Sit with each exercise, investing your full energy. You might be pleasantly surprised by the experience.

Written Example of a Seven Week Reflection Healing Schedule

Week 1:
Stare in your eyes for 1 minute without saying anything.
Do this daily

Week 2:
Stare in your eyes for 1 minute and say, "I love you."
Do this daily

Week 3:
Stare in your eyes for 2 minutes and say, "I love you."
Do this daily

Week 4:
Stare in your eyes for 3 minutes and say,
"I love you," plus your affirmations.
Do this daily

Week 5 :
Stare in your eyes for 4 minutes and say,
"I love you," plus your affirmations.
Do this daily

Week 6:
Stare in your eyes for 5 minutes and say,
"I love you," plus your affirmations.
Do this daily

Week 7:
Stare in your eyes for 5 minutes and say,
"I love you," plus your affirmations.
Do this daily

Chapter 7
Becoming Aware

Frequency Chart

How to Read the Frequency Chart

How to Utalize the Frequency Chart

"How you vibrate is what the Universe echos back to you in every moment."

Panache

Becoming Aware

"Please don't kill my vibe." "Only good vibes." These are phrases that resonate with the concept of frequency. Imagine your frequency or 'vibe' as the tuning fork of your day. It's the energetic signature you emit to the universe, signaling the experiences you're open to. Through conscious awareness, you possess the ability to swiftly shift this vibration, consequently altering your mood and the encounters that come your way.

In our expedition of personal growth and transformation, comprehending the concept of frequency stands as a formidable tool. At its essence, frequency pertains to the energetic vibrations that radiate from everything in the universe—our thoughts, emotions, and actions included. It's based on the belief that each element of existence emits a distinctive energy signature that interacts with the world around it. Becoming conscious of specific frequencies and aligning ourselves with them can fundamentally shape our experiences—within our bodies, in our interactions with others, and in our lives. Our frequency significantly influences our well-being and the reality we construct.

Consider a scenario involving the transformation of a negative interaction. Let's imagine someone faces a challenging encounter at work or in their personal life. Instead of allowing this negativity to permeate their entire day, they choose a conscious shift in their vibe. A few moments of deep breathing and self-reflection lead to a reminder of their worth and capabilities. By reframing the situation and focusing on solutions, they alter their frequency from frustration to empowerment. Had they not taken the time to consciously shift their frequency, this one situation might have disrupted their entire day.

In the daily bustle of life, many people remain unaware of their frequency, often letting their subconscious dictate the energetic tone. Recognizing one's frequency begins with developing heightened awareness. Emotions, thoughts, and actions carry unique energetic vibrations. Positive emotions such as joy, love, and gratitude emit high frequencies, while negative emotions like fear, anger, and resentment emit lower frequencies. To harness the power of frequency, it is essential to attune ourselves to these energetic signals.

Understanding and harnessing the power of frequency represents a profound stride in our voyage of personal growth. By recognizing the energy we emit and consciously aligning with higher frequencies, we unlock the potential to craft a more vibrant and fulfilling life.

This practice, when coupled with the transformative techniques explored in earlier chapters, grants us the ability to navigate change, nurture self-love, and catalyze lasting transformation. Let us delve into the art of becoming aware of our frequency and staying conscious of it throughout our journey.

On the following page, a frequency chart has been provided. This chart serves as a reference guide, aiding you in becoming aware of your frequency and guiding you toward elevating it to a more desired level. Inspired by a similar tool that significantly impacted my personal growth journey, this chart remains an invaluable resource for both my personal growth and the growth of those I share it with.

"Negativity can only affect you if you're on the same frequency. Vibe Higher"

Unknown

1000 - 700	*Enlightenment*	Source / God Consciousness
600	*Peace*	Saints & Healers
540	*Joy*	HIGHER Consciousness
500	*Love*	Heart Centered
400	**Reason**	
350	**Acceptance**	*Transformation*
310	**Willingness**	
250	**Neutrality**	*Empowered*
200	**Courage**	
175	Pride	
150	Anger	
125	Desire	*Struggle*
100	Fear	
75	Greif	
50	Apathy	*Suffering*
30	Guilt	
20	Shame	

How to read the Frequency Chart

The Frequency Chart featured on the preceding page serves as a valuable tool to gauge and elevate your emotional state. It empowers you to assess where you currently resonate emotionally, providing a roadmap to shift towards higher vibrations. Understanding and effectively utilizing this chart can significantly impact your daily experiences and interactions.

Upon examining the chart, you'll notice three columns, each holding important information:

1. **Numbers (Hertz):** These represent the frequency at which a particular emotional state resonates. It's a numerical reflection of the vibrational energy associated with that state.
2. **Words to Distinguish Resonance:** The middle column presents the emotions and states associated with each frequency. This column aids in identifying your current emotional resonance.
3. **Type of Vibration Emitted:** The far-right column signifies the type of vibration you emit into the world when resonating at a specific frequency.

While it's true that the spectrum of human emotions is vast and nuanced, we've streamlined the chart to focus on the most common and recognizable emotions. This simplification allows for a more straightforward and effective practice.

How to Utilize the Frequency Chart

By employing this process, you'll gradually find it easier to sustain a higher vibration throughout the day. The objective is to reside predominantly in the Heart Centered or higher vibrations, allowing for a more enriching and fulfilling daily experience.

1. Begin by honestly assessing your emotional state. Identify the word on the chart that best describes where you currently resonate emotionally.
2. Write down the identified word representing your current emotional state.
3. Reflect on whether you are content with your current frequency. If not, aspire to vibrate at least two levels higher on the chart.
4. Identify and note your new desired frequency. Envision how it feels to resonate at this level. List 5-10 words or feelings associated with this elevated frequency.
5. Repeatedly affirm these words, saying them aloud, and truly immerse yourself in their essence. Feel the resonance of these words throughout your being.
6. Check in with yourself periodically during the day to ensure you maintain your chosen higher frequency. If you find yourself resonating lower, revisit the affirmations, feeling and saying them aloud to recalibrate your emotional state.

Chapter 8
Transformative Practices

Sculpting a Positive Mindset

How to Practice Affirmations

Gratitude a Powerful Frequency

How to Practice It

Discovering Inner Serenity

Practicing Meditation

"We cannot become what we want by reamining what we are."

Max Depree

Transformative Practices

Life, in its beautiful complexity, unfolds as a continuous journey of growth and evolution. Amidst the bustling symphony of daily existence, the gentle whispers of our own desires and needs often get drowned out. This is where transformative practices step in, offering us a vital lifeline to reconnect with ourselves, to delve beneath the layers of routine, and rediscover the very essence of our being.

In our pursuit of personal growth, there exists a powerful unity of ingredients capable of catalyzing profound transformations within our lives. These ingredients manifest in the form of practices—small yet impactful rituals—that delicately guide us towards a deeper understanding of both ourselves and the world that surrounds us. These transformative practices, encompassing affirmations, gratitude exercises, and the art of meditation, hold within them the immense potential to illuminate our paths, reshape our mindsets, and elevate our inner well-being.

Perhaps you've heard of these practices, and maybe you've even begun to integrate them into your life. However, a question arises: Are you practicing them optimally? Let's embark on a journey to explore each of these transformative powerhouses individually, understanding their unique qualities and potentials. Subsequently, we will delve into the art of practicing them harmoniously, uncovering the magic that unfolds when they are combined—engendering incredible, sustainable change in our lives.

Sculpting a Positive Mindset

Affirmations are like seeds we plant in the fertile soil of our minds. These are positive statements meticulously crafted to reframe our thoughts and beliefs. Remember our discussion on the mind in an earlier chapter? We delved into how our brain forms neural pathways through our thoughts. Well, affirmations essentially act as these thoughts, shaping the neural landscape of our minds. They can either fuel a negative loop of self-doubt or foster a positive mindset, depending on their nature.

The Power of Belief in Affirmations

Over time, I've discovered that belief is a fundamental player in the realm of affirmations. Merely reciting an affirmation without aligning it with your genuine thoughts is like planting a seed in infertile soil—it won't flourish. For instance, standing in front of a mirror and saying, 'I'm sexy,' while internally believing, 'No one likes me' and judging the image you see reflecting back to you, won't yield the desired results. Authentic belief in what you affirm is crucial; it needs to resonate with your thoughts to create a positive neural pathway.

If you genuinely believe you're a 'sexy' and affirm this while looking in the mirror, your belief will radiate, and others will notice too. However, for affirmations that still feel like a work in progress, where belief isn't quite there yet, you need to bridge that gap.

Cultivating Belief in Your Affirmations

Aligning your affirmations with your genuine beliefs involves a process. Start by acknowledging where you stand in relation to the affirmation. If it feels far removed from your current belief system, work on adjusting it to a point where it aligns and feels realistic. Your affirmations should act as stepping stones, propelling you towards a positive mindset and empowering self-perception.

Remember, affirmations are not about wishful thinking but about creating a mental environment conducive to growth and transformation. They pave the way for a shift in mindset, fostering resilience, self-love, and confidence.

How to Practice Affirmations

Set Your Intent: Identify an area you wish to work on, whether it's self-confidence, abundance, or inner peace.

Create Your Affirmations: Create positive statements in the present tense that you believe.
For instance, *"I am confident and capable in all situations."*

Repetition and Belief: Repeat your affirmations daily, ideally in the morning or before sleep. Say them with conviction, letting them settle into your subconscious.

Example: *"I radiate love and attract positive energy into my life. I am deserving of all the good that comes my way."*

"Be careful how you talk to yourself because you are listening."

Lisa M. Hayes

Gratitude:
A Powerful Frequency

At 540 MHz, gratitude resonates at a higher frequency than love. This might seem surprising, but as Abraham's quote on the previous page suggests, many individuals use gratitude as a means to overcome their struggles. However, it's vital to recognize that this form of gratitude often carries an underlying attachment to the challenges you are facing. This attachment can inadvertently sabotage your attempts to make positive changes in their lives.

Gratitude resonating at a frequency of 540 MHz—higher than the frequency of Love is a powerful revelation when considering the transformative impact that such a simple practice can have on your personal vibration and overall life. Gratitude serves as a potent force, redirecting our focus from what may be lacking in our lives to what is abundantly present. It's the art of recognizing even the smallest blessings, nurturing a perspective of contentment and genuine appreciation.

To truly benefit from the practice of gratitude, it's essential to align it with a genuine sense of appreciation. This alignment helps release any attachment to a mindset rooted in struggle that you might be experiencing.

How to Practice Gratitude

1. **Daily Reflection**: Dedicate a few moments each day to reflect on what you're grateful for. Allow your mind to roam through your day, finding those instances that evoke a sense of gratitude.

2. **Gratitude Journal**: Maintain a gratitude journal where you jot down the things you're thankful for. This practice helps solidify the positive aspects of your life.

3. **Express Sincerity**: Don't just keep your gratitude to yourself. Express it to the people who've made a positive impact on your life. Whether through words, gestures, or deeds, let them know how appreciative you are.

Example: *"I am grateful for the supportive friendships that fill my life with joy and understanding."*

"When you feel gratitude often you are looking at a struggle that you've overcome and feeling grateful, in other words happy, that you're still not in the struggle, but you're still messing with that vibration just a little bit."

Abraham Hicks

Discovering Inner Serenity

Meditation is a sacred sanctuary we create within ourselves —a space to silence the chaos of the external world, center our thoughts, and tap into the wellspring of our inner wisdom. It's a practice of mindfulness that cultivates clarity, peace, and a profound connection with our authentic selves.

Meditation bestows an array of benefits upon those who embrace it. Regular practice has been linked to reduced stress levels, improved focus and concentration, enhanced emotional well-being, and increased self-awareness. Physiologically, it can lower blood pressure, boost the immune system, and promote better sleep. Over time, meditation becomes a powerful tool in navigating the complexities of life with a calm and centered mind.

The roots of meditation can be traced back thousands of years across various cultures and traditions. It has been an integral part of spiritual and philosophical practices in ancient civilizations such as the Indus Valley, where the earliest evidence of meditation was found in the form of wall art depicting people in meditative postures. Over centuries, meditation has been practiced in different forms in Buddhism, Hinduism, Taoism, and ancient Christian traditions. This age-old technique has withstood the test of time and is now embraced globally for its immense benefits.

There are numerous misconceptions about meditation, often leading people to believe that there's only one 'right' way to practice it. However, here's a secret: meditation is a vast landscape with diverse approaches, and you might already be meditating in ways you never recognized. Below, we'll explore a few popular methods, encouraging you to explore and choose what resonates most with your being.

Practicing Meditation

There are many different ways to practice meditation. I have listed below some of the ways you can explore meditation and find which works for you. Give yourself time when attempting meditation (about a month or so) before you decide it isnt working for you. It is a Journey, not a race.

Still Meditation:

Still meditation is usually the one people try and then give up. It simply requires one to become physically and mentally still. Find a quiet spot and sitorlay down. Focus n breath, but allow the mind to become empty, without falling asleep.

Guided Meditation:

Guided meditation involves listening to a facilitator who provides instructions or uses music to guide you through the practice. Apps, videos, or audio recordings often serve as valuable aids. They can lead you through breathing techniques, visualizations, or mindfulness exercises, making meditation more accessible, especially for beginners.

Active Meditation:

Active meditation involves integrating mindfulness into daily activities. Engage fully in a task—be it walking, exercising, journaling, creating art, or even cleaning—allowing your thoughts to dissolve into the task at hand. Focus on the sensations, movements, and details of the activity, immersing yourself completely in the present moment.

As we embrace these transformative practices, we set the stage for sculpting a vibrant future. The seeds of change we've sown through affirmations, gratitude, and meditation now beckon us towards the tangible realm of goals, habits, and routines. The introspective journey we've embarked upon equips us with newfound self-awareness and a clearer vision of the life we aspire to live. Now, let's transition our understanding from inner transformation to actionable steps that will shape our external reality.

Still Meditation

Active Meditation

Guided
Meditation

Join the Spiritual Gangsta
CommUnity on the
Anchored Soul Therapy App
and listen to
Sound Healing Meditations

"Prayer is asking for what you need and Meditation is receiving the answers."

Shannon aka The Spiritual Gangsta

Chapter 9
Creating a Vibrant Future

Setting Goals for a Vibrant Future

The Importance of Habits

Designing Supportive Routines

Creating a Vibrant Future

In this chapter, we embark on a journey to construct the very foundation of a vibrant and fulfilling future. As we've discovered in our exploration of the mind, the subconscious plays a pivotal role in our lives. To align our external reality with our internal transformation, we must create an environment that supports and nurtures these changes.

We initiate this transformative process by setting goals, for without a clear destination, our path remains obscured. Once we've defined our goals, we proceed to establish routines that act as stepping stones, guiding us toward these milestones. Within these routines, we cultivate positive habits, reinforcing our journey of change and fortifying the new neural pathways in our subconscious.

By cyclically moving through the establishment of goals, the creation of supportive routines, and the nurturing of empowering habits, we complete a profound cycle of transformation, gradually reprogramming our subconscious mind and manifesting the life we truly desire.

Setting Goals
For a Vibrant Future

Setting goals is akin to charting a roadmap for our ambitions. Goals provide direction, motivation, and a sense of purpose. They fuel our drive and inspire action. In this section, we will unravel the art of setting effective goals that align with our vision of a vibrant future. From short-term aspirations to long-term dreams, we'll learn how to structure our objectives and navigate the path toward success.

Have you heard of the SMART way to create goals? The concept of setting goals in a structured and thoughtful manner has been around for a long time, and various versions of the SMART criteria have been used in management, project planning, education, and personal development. The SMART framework gained popularity and widespread use in the business world during the 1980s and 1990s.

Different sources credit different authors or management theorists with the development and popularization of the SMART criteria. Some suggest that it emerged from the work of Peter Drucker, a well-known management consultant, educator, and author. Others attribute it to George T. Doran, a consultant and former Director of Corporate Planning for Washington Water Power Company, who wrote a paper in 1981 titled "There's a S.M.A.R.T. Way to Write Management's Goals and Objectives.

Regardless of its specific origin, the SMART criteria have become a valuable tool for setting meaningful and achievable goals in various settings, helping individuals and organizations improve their planning and performance. Let's learn the SMART way.

1. **Be Specific (S):** Define your goal clearly and specifically. It should answer the questions: What do I want to accomplish? Why is it important? Who is involved? Where will it happen? What are the limitations?
2. **Measurable (M):** Make your goal measurable so you can track your progress and stay motivated. Ask questions like: How much? How many? How will I know when the goal is achieved?
3. **Achievable (A):** Ensure that your goal is realistic and attainable within the given resources and constraints. Consider your current circumstances, skills, and resources. Stretch yourself, but set goals that are possible.
4. **Relevant (R):** Your goal should align with your overall objectives and be relevant to your life or work. Ensure that it's meaningful and worth your time and effort.
5. **Time-bound (T):** Set a deadline to create a sense of urgency and commitment. Define when you want to achieve the goal. This prevents procrastination and provides a sense of accountability.

Now that you know how to properly set a goal, let's get into how you can make them achievable, because having a goal in mind is only the first step. The steps listed below are some proven ways to go from having an idea of a goal to actually acheiving the goal.

1. **Write Them Down:** Document your goals in a place where you can review them regularly. Writing down your goals makes them more tangible and reinforces your commitment.
2. **Break Down Your Goals:** Divide large, complex goals into smaller, manageable tasks. Each task should be achievable in a shorter time frame. This helps maintain motivation and gives a sense of progress.
3. **Create an Action Plan:** Outline the specific steps you'll take to achieve each goal. This helps you stay organized and focused on the tasks necessary for success.
4. **Stay Flexible:** Understand that circumstances might change, and you might need to adapt your goals accordingly. Be open to reassessing and adjusting your goals as needed.
5. **Monitor and Evaluate:** Regularly review your progress. Celebrate your achievements and learn from any setbacks. Adjust your goals and action plans if needed to stay on track.
6. **Stay Committed and Stay Positive:** Stay committed to your goals, maintain a positive mindset, and believe in your ability to achieve them. Visualize your success and keep pushing forward.

"Setting goals is the first step in turning the invisible into the visible"

Tony Robbins

The Importance of Habits

In 2011, after a disastrous episode around my 2010 birthday that left me bewildered at how I had survived, I knew I had to quit drinking, even if only for 30 days. Recollecting that time, I understood I needed to steer clear of certain events and social circles if I genuinely desired this change. I had to introspect about my relationship with drinking—how I used it to relax or have a good time—and identify the social triggers influencing this behavior. Sometimes, the key to changing habits lies in altering our social environments. Staying away from these triggers was crucial for my success in quitting drinking. I explored fresh ways to socialize and unwind without relying on alcohol. Staying consistent for 30 days, a goal I had set for myself, helped me recognize that this was a negative habit I no longer wanted to embrace. Instead, I forged a new positive habit.

Identifying the triggers of my negative habit enabled me to substitute them with positive alternatives. I commenced with a modest goal of not drinking for 30 days, reminding myself of the reasons behind this decision—primarily, battling depression and rectifying my behavior when under the influence. I rewarded myself for every achievement, be it a day or a week without drinking, with dinners, enjoyable events, and words of affirmation.

The journey to establish this habit wasn't a smooth ride; my commitment was tested several times. One instance that stands out was when a friend invited me to a party. I was excited about the gathering, having already been three weeks into my goal. I felt no inclination to drink at that point. However, upon informing her that I wouldn't be drinking, she abruptly withdrew the invitation, stating I couldn't attend if I wasn't going to drink. I was bewildered. Why would my own friends not want me around if I chose not to drink? I knew I was a kinder and more pleasant person when sober. She expressed concern that I might relapse, but I didn't have a drinking problem; I was striving to better myself and my habits. This incident strained our relationship, and I began to realize that she had unwittingly held me accountable. Who knows what would have transpired at that party? That 30 day goal turned into 5 years of sobriety.

After five years, I attempted to reintroduce alcohol into my life. However, that endeavor was short-lived, and as I write this book, I am nearing another five years of sobriety. Looking back, I now understand that friend, despite the rift our relationship experienced, inadvertently played a crucial role in my accountability during those early stages of change. Habits sculpt our character, influence our choices, and mold our triumphs. Empowering habits act as propellers towards our goals, ensuring success becomes a steady companion on our journey.

Habits are deeply ingrained behaviors, gradually become automatic through repetition, often in specific contexts. Understanding the psychology of habits is key to leveraging their transformative potential in our lives. Habits typically originate from a series of repeated events—a trigger initiates a behavior, followed by a reward or a form of satisfaction, and this loop reinforces itself, ultimately forming a habit. It's crucial to recognize that these habits can be either positive or negative, hence, maintaining mindfulness about the habits we are forming is essential.

Several elements contribute to the formation of habits, including consistency, emotional connection, environment, and social circumstances. My personal experience of overcoming a negative habit sheds light on the transformative power of altering our environment and social circle to induce positive habit changes. By staying consistent with a goal of not drinking for 30 days, it was possible to break the negative habit of excessive drinking, ultimately creating a positive, lasting change.

In the following segment, I've outlined the psychology of habits, by understanding how they form, how to recognize them and what influences habits to be created, you will be able to create better habits to support you in moving forward towards the life you desire.

Understanding how habits form –
key comp recogn

Cue: A trigger initiating the behavior, which could be a specific time, place, emotion, preceding action, or a person.

Routine: The behavior itself, encompassing physical, mental, or emotional actions.

Reward: The positive outcome or satisfaction derived from the behavior, reinforcing the habit loop.

Repetition: As the loop solidifies through repetition, the habit becomes more automatic and deeply ingrained.

Habit Influences:

Consistency: Regularity and repetition play pivotal roles in forming a habit. The more consistent the behavior, the quicker it solidifies into a habit.

Emotional Connection: Emotions associated with a habit, whether positive or negative, can amplify its formation and strength.

Environmental Cues: Factors in the environment, like a particular place or object, can trigger associated habits.

Social Influences: The people around us and societal norms can significantly influence our habits.

Cultivating Empowering Habits

When we are wanting to create new habits to support change in our lives, we need to first be able to recognize the cues that prompt current habits, these are also considered triggers. Awareness to these triggers will mark the initial steps we need to take towards change. With this awareness we then can begin to replace the unwanted habits by substituting undesirable habits with constructive ones triggered by the same cues, fostering positive change.

Let's look back at my experience of quitting drinking. I became aware that whenever my friends called me to hang out we wen drinking, always. I identified that I even had the urge to drink prior to meeting up with them to "save money," but when I got honey with myself and looked at the truth, I was having social anxiety. I was insecure of going out alone. So I needed to replace the habit of drinking prior to me going out and gain confidence in me going out alone.

This bring me to the next steps, start small. Initiate your change with manageable habits to create confidence and gain momentum. In order for me to create this change I knew I needed to be able to go out alone with condfidence so i could then go meet friend with confidence. In order to do this, I started small and began by going to dinner alone. I had massive anxiety about going out to dinner alone so I had to think of a way to keep me distracted, and no, smartphones were not as popular as they are now, so when I went out to eat I brought a book to read and keep me distracted from thinking everyone was looking at me. I continued to be patient and persistent, knowing that this negative habit I was breaking was going to take time and I needed to be devoted to myself if I wanted this change. Below are the ways to ensure your success in cultivating new habits.

Identify Triggers: Recognize the cues that prompt current habits. Awareness marks the initial stride towards change.

Replace Unwanted Habits: Substitute undesirable habits with constructive ones triggered by the same cues, fostering positive change.

Start Small: Initiate with manageable habits to bolster confidence and gain momentum for more substantial changes.

Visual Reminders: Employ visual cues to serve as a constant reminder of the habit you're striving to nurture.

Accountability: Share your habit goals with a friend or mentor who can provide encouragement and hold you accountable, enhancing your commitment.

Celebrate Progress: Acknowledge and celebrate your achievements, reinforcing the reward aspect of habit formation and motivating further progress.

Patience and Persistence: Recognize that habit change is a gradual process demanding effort and dedication. Persevere through setbacks and keep striving towards your goals.

Understanding the psychology of habits equips us to consciously shape our behaviors in alignment with our aspirations, steering us towards a life that is more fulfilling and purpose-driven. Here are a few suggestions on how to incorporate habits conducive to growth and weel-being into your daily life.

Regular Exercise: Enhances physical and mental health, contributing to overall well-being.

Mindfulness and Meditation: Cultivate presence, reduce stress, and sharpen focus, fostering a more balanced and peaceful state of mind.

Reading: Facilitates knowledge acquisition, empathy, and cognitive development, nurturing continual personal growth.

Gratitude Practice: Cultivates a positive mindset, improving mental health and fostering a more appreciative outlook on life.

Healthy Eating: Nourishes the body, promoting well-being and ensuring sustained energy levels.

"You'll never change your life until you change something you do daily. The secret of your success is found in your daily routine."

John C. Maxwell

Designing
Supportive Routines

BUILDING

The blaring alarm jolts you from your slumber, initiating a frenzied race to jumpstart the day. Instead of promptly rising, the tempting allure of news updates and social media notifications draws you in.

In an instant, you startle, realizing time has slipped through your fingers. Adrenaline surges, propelling you into a hurried attempt to get ready. Hair hastily brushed, a fleeting glance in the mirror, and off you go. Breakfast, once a cornerstone of a healthy start, is now replaced by a hasty grab-and-go from a popular fast-food joint, leaving your body and mind far from nourished.

The frantic rush continues as you dive into the morning traffic, surrounded by irate drivers whose frustration mirrors your own. Road rage, an unwelcome companion, sets a tense tone for the day ahead.

In the clamor of our modern lives, we often hear about the importance of routines, especially in the morning, to set a positive tone for the day. However, this isn't a book to remind you to wake up at 5 am and run 10 miles for productivity and health. Beyond the whirlwind of rushed mornings, there's a deeper issue we need to explore—the cycle of emotional avoidance.

The Cycle of Emotional Avoidance

In a bustling city, there lived Sarah, a woman who had endured the emotional turmoil of a past relationship. Each morning, her alarm chimed, heralding the start of a new day. Sarah, however, dreaded the beginning of each morning, not due to the daily tasks, but because it meant confronting her emotions.

As she awoke, she would instinctively reach for her phone, scrolling through social media. This digital diversion was her way of avoiding the memories that lay just beneath the surface. The comments and likes became a form of validation, temporarily soothing the ache in her heart.

In the mirror, she would put on a façade, painting a portrait of happiness to disguise the true struggle within. The reflection in the mirror seemed like a distant acquaintance, a representation of the person she wished to be, rather than a true reflection of herself.

As the day progressed, she would convince herself that she had moved on, ignoring the emotional wounds that still festered. Every mention of love, relationships, or heartache was met with a casual dismissal, saying, "It doesn't bother me anymore." But the unease in her voice and the tension in her shoulders betrayed her true feelings.

"First forget inspiration. Habit is more dependable. Habit will sustain you weather youre inspired or not."

Octavia Butler

Empowering Sarah Through Deliberate Routines

In our bustling, modern world, routines are not just about habituated actions; they can be intentional, compassionate tools for managing emotions and fostering healing. Let's reimagine Sarah's story, demonstrating how she could have employed purposeful routines to navigate her emotional landscape.

As Sarah's alarm rings, she takes a deep breath, acknowledging that the day has begun. Instead of reaching for her phone to numb her feelings with the digital world, she reaches for a journal on her bedside table. Here, in the sacred pages of her journal, she begins to unravel her thoughts and emotions, setting the tone for a day of mindful awareness.

Her reflection in the mirror is now met with self-compassion. She affirms herself, reminding that healing is a journey, and she embraces both her strengths and vulnerabilities. Each brushstroke through her hair becomes a moment of self-care, a reminder that she is worthy of love and gentleness.

Throughout the day, Sarah keeps her feelings at the forefront. She has planned moments to check in with herself— short breaks to breathe, meditate, or take a walk. During these times, she allows her emotions to surface, acknowledging them without judgment. This deliberate approach allows her to process and gradually heal the wounds of her past. As the day unfolds, she engages in activities that nurture her soul—a nourishing breakfast, meaningful conversations, and engaging in creative pursuits that fuel her passion. In the evening, she doesn't shy away from her emotions. Instead, she embraces them, perhaps seeking support from a trusted friend, therapist, or support group.

This intentional, emotionally connected routine has become Sarah's anchor. It doesn't stifle her emotions; it gives her the space and structure to face them with grace and courage. It supports her in healing from the inside out, honoring her emotional journey and encouraging growth.

By Sarah being able to stay emotionally connected n conscious of her thoughts she is creating a day full of presence and awareness so she will be able to actively choose her thoughts, feelings and actions creating a day she chooses to enjoy. She can also become aware of the thought, feelings and actions keeping her in separation consciousness from the life she desires to have.

"Mindset, Habits, and Routines are the building blocks for success."

Unknown

Your Routine for a Fulfilling Life

In the quest for healing, growth, and a life steeped in alignment, a thoughtfully designed daily routine can be your steadfast companion. Let's look and compare a few example routines to help navigate through the insights and tools you've encountered in this transformative journey, translating them into tangible actions that shape a vibrant and purposeful day.

Rising Mindfulness:

- Mindful Wake-up: Gently awaken and resist the temptation of immediate digital engagement.

- Breath Awareness: Spend a few minutes focusing on your breath, grounding yourself for the day.

- Frequency Check-in: Begin with deciding where on the frequency chart you want to be and formulate what that feels like to you.

- Affirmations: Affirm the type of day you will have using the frequency as a foundation of your affirmations.

- Gratitude Practice: Begin with gratitude, acknowledging the positive aspects of your how your day will be.

- Mirror Affirmations: Take a moment to look in the mirror and affirm love and acceptance for yourself.

- Act of Nourishment: Prepare and enjoy a wholesome breakfast, considering it an act of self-care and nourishment.

Mid-day Check-ins:
- Reflection Time: Through out the day set aside moments to reflect on your emotional state and document any potential triggers, thoughts, and emotions.

- Mindful Responses: Practice responding to triggers using the methods described in the book to mindfully aim for constructive and healing reactions.

- Mid-day Check-in: Pause to reassess your goals and aspirations, realigning your actions accordingly.

- Frequency Check-in: Take time though out the day to check in with yourself and see where your emotional state is at, resetting as needed through your affirmations for the day.

- Goal Realignment: Review and adjust your daily goals to align with your broader life objectives.

- Healthy Habits: Practice one new healthy habit that supports your goals and overall well-being.

Evening Observations and Integration
- Journaling: Write down your reflections on the day, recognizing areas of growth and areas for improvement. Brain Dump if needed.

- Meditation: End the day with a meditation

- Gratitude Practice: Conclude your day with gratitude, appreciating the experiences and lessons.

In crafting this routine, remember that flexibility and adaptability are key. Tailor this daily plan to suit your individual preferences and lifestyle while adhering to the principles outlined in this transformative journey. Through consistent practice and conscious effort, this routine can be the beacon that guides you towards a life that resonates with your true self.

"Whatever the present moment contains, accept it as if you had chosen it. Always work with it, no against it"

Eckhart Tolle

Chapter 10
Tips

Affirmations for Transformation

Journal Prompts for Shadow Work

Affirmations for Transformation

In the following section, you will discover a range of affirmation suggestions aligned with the frequency chart previously discussed. These affirmations serve as a helpful resource if you're facing difficulty generating affirmations on your own.

Moreover, these affirmations are designed not only to aid you in shifting your current mindset but also to facilitate a transition from lower frequencies to higher, more positive ones.

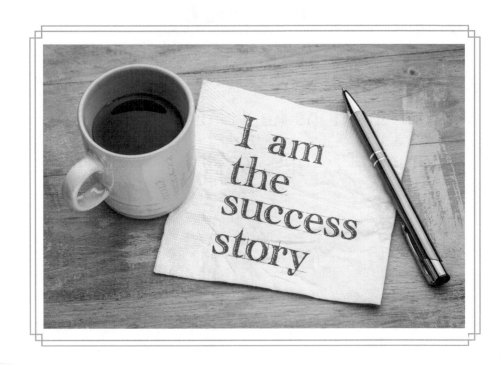

Peace, Joy, Love

HIGHER
Consciousness
Heart Centered

Love, joy, and peace are
emotions that I experience
regularly, which allows me to
be an embodiment of love.

Transformation

Reason
Acceptance
Willingness

I am exactly where I need to be.
I am on the right path.
I improve every day.

Empowered

Neutrality
Courage

I am capable of achieving anything I set
my mind to.
I am confident in my abilities and trust
myself to make the right decisions.

Struggle

Pride
Anger
Desire
Fear

I let go of anger & offer forgiveness.
I am fully capable.
I am doing better every day.

Suffering

Greif
Apathy
Guilt
Shame

I let go of _ _ _ _.
I love and approve of myself.
I am safe and all is well.

Journal Prompts for Shadow Work

While triggers often propel us into the realm of our shadow selves, there are times when our consciousness takes us willingly on this introspective journey. For those moments when we feel ready to delve into our hidden depths without the prodding of triggers, journaling can be an incredibly powerful tool. It allows us to shine a light on the darker corners of our psyche, illuminating what lies hidden.

Below you will find some thought-provoking journal prompts to guide you in this process of self-exploration and shadow integration. You can use these when you need some inspiration for your journaling or when you feel ready to dive deeper into your Subconcious mind.

Journal Prompts

- What labels or identifiers do I have about myself?
Do you believe them to be true? Are they from yourself or are they from others?

- What aspects of my personality do I find most difficult to accept?

- How does the inner voice in my head sound?

- What are some of my shadow traits and how do they manifest in my life?

- What are some of the ways I seek external validation to avoid facing my shadow?

- What are 5 ways I have changed in the past 5 years? Why or why not? Are they positive changes?

- How have I been getting in my own way lately?

- What are some unconscious patterns or behaviors that cause me harm?

- What are some of my negative self-talk patterns and how do they impact my life?

- What does showing up authentically look like?

- What unconscious beliefs do I have about myself?

- How would I describe myself to a stranger?

- How has my perception of myself evolved?

- Do I feel jealousy or envy towards others? If so, why?

- Is there anyone I hold anger, hostility or hate red towards?

"Gratitude is the frequency as if something is already here. Express gratitude to all the things you have and desire to experience change in your life."

Unknown

Chapter 11
Putting It All Together

Integration and Application of Learnings

Integrating Change

Now that we've explored the impact of our past on our present and empowered ourselves with strategies to actively shape our lives, it's time to unify these insights and initiate tangible changes, steering our lives toward fulfillment and growth.

To streamline this transformative journey, divide the day into two fundamental parts: Rising Observations, symbolizing new beginnings, and Evening Reflections, signifying reflection and closure. These anchor points will facilitate a smoother integration of healthy daily habits, allowing you to witness and appreciate changes more swiftly.

As we approach the end of this book, I want to acknowledge you for your commitment to personal growth and healing. The journey you've embarked upon is not always easy, and it takes incredible courage to face your shadow, heal your wounds, and transform your life. You've come a long way, and now, it's time to think about how you can integrate everything you've learned into your daily life.

It's crucial to recognize that this spiritual healing journey isn't a one-size-fits-all approach. Tailor your approach to suit your unique preferences and circumstances, ensuring that your comfort doesn't lead to stagnation. Embrace the discomfort that change might initially bring, for it often precedes a sense of excitement and progress. If it's propelling you toward growth and a better version of yourself, then you're undoubtedly on the right path.

Embracing Integration: Bridging the Gap

Integration is the bridge that connects personal growth and transformation to your everyday existence. It's about taking the insights you've gained, the healing you've experienced, and the tools you've acquired and applying them in your day-to-day life. This process is where true change happens.

During this journey, you've examined your past, your traumas, and your innermost fears. You've explored your emotional landscape, uncovered the roots of your habits and behaviors, and begun the process of rewriting your story. But none of this truly matters unless it finds its way into your daily actions and choices.

The Awakening to the Spiritual Gangsta Within Workbook: Your 90-Day Transformation Companion

In this book, I've shared my story and a roadmap to help you begin your transformation journey. However, lasting change requires time, practice, and ongoing guidance. This is where my workbook comes in.

I'm thrilled to introduce my companion workbook, designed to take you through a 90-day transformation. In these pages, you'll find more insights, exercises, and practical tips to support you in your ongoing journey. This workbook isn't just a collection of exercises; it's a personalized guide that builds upon the foundation you've laid here.

Whether you're looking to deepen your shadow work, further develop healthy routines, or maintain the momentum you've built, the workbook provides a structured path for your continued growth and healing. It's a place to journal your progress, set meaningful goals, and track your transformation as you move through each day.

By investing in this workbook, you're investing in yourself and your future. It's a tangible, supportive companion that will help you stay on track and aligned with your true self, long after you've turned the final page of this book.

Remember, the journey doesn't end here; it continues as you apply what you've learned and experienced to create a more fulfilling life. Your path to healing and transformation is an ongoing process, and I'm excited to offer you a tool that will walk with you every step of the way.

Thank you for joining me on this journey of self-discovery, healing, and transformation. I hope you decide to take the next step with the workbook, and I look forward to supporting you as you continue to grow and create the life you truly deserve.

With love and gratitude,
Shannon
   aka The Spiritual Gangsta

Connect. Reflect. Transform. Transcend.

AnchoredSoulTherapy.com

Made in the USA
Columbia, SC
22 March 2024

33140921R00120